W9-APZ-143

ALEX RODRIGUEZ

ALEX RODRIGUEZ

A Biography

Wayne Stewart

GREENWOOD BIOGRAPHIES

GREENWOOD PRESS
WESTPORT, CONNECTICUT•LONDON

Library of Congress Cataloging-in-Publication Data

Stewart, Wayne, 1951-
  Alex Rodriguez : a biography / Wayne Stewart.
    p. cm. — (Greenwood biographies, ISSN 1540–4900)
  Includes bibliographical references and index.
  ISBN–13: 978–0–313–33975–2 (alk. paper)
  ISBN–10: 0–313–33975–9 (alk. paper)
  1. Rodriguez, Alex, 1975- 2. Baseball players—United
States—Biography.   I. Title.
  GV865.R623S83   2007
  796.357092—dc22
  [B]   2007009606

British Library Cataloguing in Publication Data is available.

Library of Congress Catalog Card Number: 2007009606
ISBN–13: 978–0–313–33975–2
ISBN–10: 0–313–33975–9
ISSN: 1540–4900

First published in 2007

Greenwood Press, 88 Post Road West, Westport, CT 06881
An imprint of Greenwood Publishing Group, Inc.
www.greenwood.com

Printed in the United States of America

The paper used in this book complies with the
Permanent Paper Standard issued by the National
Information Standards Organization (Z39.48-1984).

10 9 8 7 6 5 4 3 2 1

To the ones that matter the most, family.

CONTENTS

Photo essay follows page 81.

SERIES FOREWORD

In response to high school and public library needs, Greenwood developed this distinguished series of full-length biographies specifically for student use. Prepared by field experts and professionals, these engaging biographies are tailored for high school students who need challenging yet accessible biographies. Ideal for secondary school assignments, the length, format, and subject areas are designed to meet educators' requirements and students' interests.

Greenwood offers an extensive selection of biographies spanning all curriculum related subject areas including social studies, the sciences, literature and the arts, history and politics, as well as popular culture, covering public figures and famous personalities from all time periods and backgrounds, both historic and contemporary, who have made an impact on American and/or world culture. Greenwood biographies were chosen based on comprehensive feedback from librarians and educators. Consideration was given to both curriculum relevance and inherent interest. The result is an intriguing mix of the well known and the unexpected, the saints and sinners from long-ago history and contemporary pop culture. Readers will find a wide array of subject choices from fascinating crime figures like Al Capone to inspiring pioneers like Margaret Mead, from the greatest minds of our time like Stephen Hawking to the most amazing success stories of our day like J. K. Rowling.

While the emphasis is on fact, not glorification, the books are meant to be fun to read. Each volume provides in-depth information about the subject's life from birth through childhood, the teen years, and adulthood.

A thorough account relates family background and education, traces personal and professional influences, and explores struggles, accomplishments, and contributions. A timeline highlights the most significant life events against a historical perspective. Bibliographies supplement the reference value of each volume.

INTRODUCTION

When Alex Rodriguez was born on July 27, 1975, in New York City to Victor and Lourdes, they gave their third child the full name of Alexander Emmanuel Rodriguez. His parents were natives of the Dominican Republic, a country known for its burning climate and its equally fervid love of baseball. As a matter of fact, Victor had played baseball there professionally as a catcher, and he passed on his interest in the game to Alex.

Thus, by the time Alex was two, he was already in love with the game of baseball, although at that stage he was interested only in the hitting phase of the game, wielding a plastic bat his father had given him, and doing so with authority—it was not uncommon for him to drill the ball so hard he broke items in his family's Manhattan shoe store.

A few years later, the family, due to assiduous work—his mother labored in an automobile assembly factory while his father ran the shoe business—had scrimped enough to afford to move back to the Dominican Republic. When Alex was only eight, however, the country's poor economic conditions caused them to lose a store they were running, interrupting what had been an idyllic life there. Victor once more uprooted his family, and it was off to Miami for the Rodriguezes.

In the United States, Alex struggled with his English and, by extension, his schooling, but in a fairly short period of time he adjusted. In the meantime, more of his early baseball influences began to take shape. He studied big-league players on television with a maturity far beyond his age. Then, when he met Juan Arteaga, a coach of a local team, he joined his first organized league. Later, another coach, Eddie Rodriguez (no relation to Alex) would, like Arteaga, become a mentor to this bud-ding baseball star.

Not long after turning nine, Alex was devastated when his father aban-doned his family. Alex, shattered, at first refused to believe Victor was gone for good, but he soon grew to realize the truth. A divorce later placed a blunt exclamation mark to his realization.

At that point, his mother became even more vital in his life. She took charge of the family, worked three jobs to stave off utter poverty, and de-terminedly instilled in Alex the values he would cling to for the rest of his life—values such as taking intense pride in one's work and doing it with the constant goal of perfection.

The family survived but did not thrive, and Lourdes could not afford to send Alex to a private school that seemed perfect for his aspirations. But with help from Arteaga and the school, Westminster Christian High School in Miami, Alex enrolled there and became a member of the pow-erhouse baseball team. At that point, yet another mentor emerged, Rich Hofman, the coach of the Westminster Warriors squad.

By Alex's junior year, eight of the nine starters on Hofman's team were destined to play professional baseball, four at the big-league level. Alex, though not flawless, displayed signs of early greatness, propelling 400-foot homers while hitting a proverbial ton (.477) and being ubiquitous as a base runner with an on-base percentage of almost .600. The team stormed its way to a national championship with a 33–2 record. In his senior year, he hit a scintillating .505 and fulfilled Coach Hofman's prophecy of a few years earlier when he became the number one draft pick in the country, gobbled up by the Seattle Mariners. When he signed his first contract, a relatively modest financial future seemed secure, but the $1.3 million deal that he inked was only a taste of what was to come.

His first year in pro ball, 1994, was a whirlwind, with Alex not only making his minor-league debut but getting his first taste of big-league ball as well—all by the age of just 18. His ascension to greatness did not take long. In 1996, during his first full big-league season, he was named to the American League All-Star team, and by season's end it had been a case of, as they say, "lights out." That year's offensive outburst remains one of the greatest hitting displays in the annals of the game, certainly the greatest ever by a shortstop, claimed many experts. He led the league in hitting with a lusty .358 batting average and set numerous highs for a major-league shortstop, including the most doubles, hits, runs, and slug-ging percentage. He was a veritable baseball wunderkind.

Just two years later, he became only the third man to combine super-lative speed with power to the tune of stealing 40 or more bases while blasting 40-plus home runs. Fast-forward another two years to 2000 and, by baseball standards, an earth-shattering event took place when the man universally known as A-Rod signed a 10-year deal with the Texas Rangers calling for a total salary of $252 million! It was a contract that would change Rodriguez's life forever.

Like a fable with the moral, "Be careful what you wish for," Rodriguez's tale was replete not only with his becoming the highest paid player in baseball, but also of three years of unbridled personal success in Texas coupled, contrastingly, with abysmal failure for the team and, in many ways most strikingly, a new image for A-Rod. Due largely to fans' displeasure with the greed of the game and not just an iota of jealousy, Rodriguez became the symbol of avarice and the target of much criticism and even abuse (see chapters 2 and 8). By 2006, he saw himself as a despised figure.

Certainly when he became a New York Yankee in 2004 he felt a rising discontent as it was not enough to make the playoffs there; success was defined only by winning the World Series.

Therefore, when he did not do well in clutch playoff situations, he became vilified in New York. It was readily apparent that all the money in the world would not buy a World Series ring or the adulation of unforgiving fans.

Indeed, his first three Yankee years were turbulent; he copped the 2005 MVP Award then, just one year later, despite putting up some productive numbers during the 2006 regular season, hit the nadir of his career when he disappeared in the playoffs, his bat having been rendered impotent. The stunning blow to his pride and ego came when he was inserted into the number eight hole in the lineup in game four. Imagine, the game's highest paid player ever hitting in the slot reserved for players considered to be among the weakest in the game.

Admire him or detest him, it is quite apparent that, on a diamond, he is indisputably among baseball's immortals. Should he continue to put up numbers at the pace he has—and, through 2006, there is no reason to assume he cannot continue his streak of excellence—he should stand at or near the head of the all-time lists for offensive achievements such as homers and runs driven in. He is *that* good; he will rank up there with the Hank Aarons and the Babe Ruths of the game.

Rodriguez, the product of a broken home, remains a complex figure, and, due largely to his father's having cast his family off like so much debris, Alex is wary, distrustful of those he does not know. At the same time, he is highly loyal to those who knew him before his days of stardom. Insulated with a circle of friends, he is difficult to approach, almost impossible to get to know. He guards his privacy with Brinks armored car intensity.

Some see a *Stepford Wives* facade about Rodriguez, as he seldom displays negativity even when he has been soundly attacked or criticized.

For the preparation of this book, the author, over the course of a year, had the cooperation of many wonderfully helpful people, and a special thanks is due to all the men who granted interviews, especially Tom Grieve, Bill Hofman, Bill Henderson, Eddie Rodriguez, Carlos Lezcano, and Alex Rodriguez-Roig.

It should also be noted that the office of Rodriguez's agent was repeatedly contacted in an effort to set up a brief phone interview with Rodriguez, but nothing materialized. In fact, several of his friends and former teachers either did not return phone calls or were very guarded and refused to cooperate, saying that to do so might displease Rodriguez, despite assurances that any questions about him would be innocuous.

Aside from his private nature, the most salient features of this man, strong and proud like his mother, may well be his drive—he is a perfectionist whose goal is to become the greatest player in the history of baseball—and his munificence—his donations of both time and money to causes such as the Boys and Girls Clubs go far beyond those of even the most generous of athletes.

As for his future, no one can know if he will make it to a World Series winner's circle, but one destination is inevitable: a trek to upstate New York for his eventual induction into the National Baseball Hall of Fame five years after he last laces up his spikes.

TIMELINE: CHRONOLOGY OF ALEX RODRIGUEZ'S LIFE AND CAREER

1975   Alexander Emmanuel Rodriguez is born in New York City, the third child of parents Victor and Lourdes.

1976   The Seattle Mariners franchise is born; Rodriguez's fate would later link up with this team.

1979   His family, having scrimped, saves enough money to move back to his parents' native land, the Dominican Republic.

1983   The poor economy of the Dominican Republic forces the Rodriguez family to move to Miami, where Alex will first play serious, organized baseball.

1984   Alex's father abandons his family; a divorce follows and leaves young Alex devastated.

1990   As a freshman at Christopher Columbus Catholic High School, Alex makes the varsity basketball team.

1992–1993   As a junior, then as a senior, at Westminster Christian High School, Alex's athletic statistics glisten. He stars in several sports and hits a ton in baseball and helps guide his team to a national championship. He is named the USA Baseball Junior Player of the Year.

1993   The first player selected in baseball's June draft is Rodriguez, by the Seattle Mariners.

1994   He makes his debut not only as a professional ballplayer, breaking in with the Appleton Foxes, but also as a major leaguer, debuting against the Red Sox.

1995   Rodriguez gets more minor-league seasoning and goes
        on to be named the Most Exciting Player in the Pa-
        cific Coast League.

1996   In his first full big-league season, Rodriguez makes
        it to the All-Star Game and goes on to lead the
        American League in hitting (.358), doubles (54) runs
        (141), and RBIs.(123) He also cracks 36 homers and
        establishes new records by a shortstop for runs, hits,
        doubles, extra base hits, and slugging percentage. In
        short, this season is generally considered to be the
        greatest year ever by a shortstop.

1998   A-Rod joins only two other men as the only big
        leaguers ever to accumulate 40 or more stolen bases
        and 40-plus home runs in a single season. He founds
        the Alex Rodriguez Foundation.

1999   Rodriguez slumps to .285, his lowest average for a full
        season in the majors, but still manages 42 homers.

2000   With 132 RBIs, he begins a streak of three seasons
        in which he will drive in 409 runs while averaging
        50 home runs per year. After the season, free agent
        Rodriguez is amply rewarded for his stellar diamond
        success, signing the highest contract in the history of
        sports, $252 million over his 10-year pact with the
        Texas Rangers.

2001   Rodriguez leads the American League in homers with
        52, runs scored (133), and total bases. He is only the
        fourth shortstop ever to lead his league in homers
        and the fifth youngest slugger to reach 200 lifetime
        homers.

2002   After winning his first Gold Glove Award, Rodriguez
        marries Cynthia Scurtis during the off-season. Al-
        though he also is named the Player of the Year by the
        prestigious poll of his peers conducted by the Sport-
        ing News, he is denied the American League Most
        Valuable Player Award despite his league-leading 57
        home runs, a new high by a shortstop, and his league
        leadership in RBIs and total bases. He donates $3.9
        million to the University of Miami to fund an annual
        scholarship for a Boys and Girls Club member and to
        help fund a renovation program for the UM baseball
        stadium.

2003   Despite laboring for a last-place Texas Rangers club, Rodriguez cops his first American League MVP trophy. He becomes the youngest player ever to reach the 300 home run circle. For the third consecutive year, he leads the league in home runs. Further, with six consecutive seasons of 40-plus home runs, only Babe Ruth (with seven) topped A-Rod in this realm.

2004   Rodriguez, amid a swirl of publicity, is courted by the Boston Red Sox but winds up signing with the New York Yankees. In addition, he becomes a father, adding daughter Natasha to his family.

2005   Rodriguez becomes the youngest player ever to reach the 400 home run strata. On a personal note, he publicly announces he is attending therapy sessions, doing so in the hope of letting youngsters realize they should be unafraid to ask for help in their personal life.

2006   Frustrations abound as boos tumble over A-Rod and the Yankees bow out after the American League Division Series.

Chapter 1

RODRIGUEZ'S
ROOTS, 1975–1993

Born Alexander Emmanuel Rodriguez, the man who would later gain one-name celebrity status as A-Rod began life on July 27, 1975, as a native New Yorker, joining a sister, Susy, and his brother Joe. His parents were Victor and Lourdes (née Navarro) Rodriguez, both proud natives of the Dominican Republic, a country about half the size of Indiana, that "shares the island that Columbus called Hispaniola with Haiti," a land that experienced its first taste of baseball in 1891, brought there by two brothers from Cuba who set up two teams that played in Santo Domingo, the city in which Alex would later spend considerable time as a boy.[1]

When Rodriguez was born, the Age of Aquarius, which had dawned several years earlier, was gone, but former Beatles member Paul McCartney made headlines when he was fined for growing marijuana. The video cassette recorder was introduced, in both the VHS and Betamax formats, but few people owned one—a blank tape ran in the neighborhood of $20. Future golf standout Tiger Woods was born that year and so was a company called Microsoft.

Alex's first residence was in Manhattan, nestled behind the shoe store his parents owned and ran. Because he moved at a very young age, however, the man who would later be featured regularly in New York tabloids has few memories of his early days in the Big Apple.

When he was just two years of age, his father gave him a plastic bat along with a rubber ball, and soon Alex was taking vicious little cuts inside the household and out. It was not at all unusual for him to break things in the family store. Long before his early days in pro ball when he would experience some problems with pitch selection, Rodriguez recalled that he would take a swat at any pitch that seemed tempting.

His parents labored hard and long, with his father selling shoes and babysitting the children; his mother left for work at 4:00 A.M. to make her trek to a job at an automobile assembly factory. By the time Alex reached the age of four, his parents had, after much toil, achieved their great American dream; they had managed to squirrel away enough money to make the move back to the Dominican Republic. This was an ambition for many Dominicans living in New York City's Washington Heights neighborhoods.

The Dominican Republic was the perfect stomping ground for a future baseball star. After all, it was the birthplace of legends, a hotbed of talent that had churned out such greats as Juan Marichal, Rico Carty, Pedro Guerrero, Felipe Alou, and his brothers Jesus and Matty and would later produce stars such as Moises Alou, Albert Pujols, Pedro Martinez, Manny Ramirez, Vladimir Guerrero, David Ortiz, Sammy Sosa, Alfonso Soriano, and countless others. The nation is to major league baseball as the Atlantic Coast Conference is to the National Basketball Association.

Further, if the Dominican Republic is a baseball hub, then the town of San Pedro de Macoris, which fed big-league baseball a host of shortstops, is the mecca. A billboard that sits outside the town proclaims, "Welcome to San Pedro de Maoris, the City Which Has Given the Most Major Leaguers to the World." The style of play there came to be labeled *beisbol romantico,* characterized by intense hustle, constantly trying to generate an edge, an advantage, on both offense and defense.

In 1947, when Brooklyn Dodgers star Jackie Robinson shattered the color barrier and big-league baseball finally, long overdue, opened its doors to African Americans, baseball owners also began to scout the Caribbean islands more intently. Previously, because a majority of Dominicans' ancestry could be traced back to include some African slaves—the country was rich in multiracial diversity—baseball refused to sign those they knew were "colored" players.

At any rate, the Rodriguezes, now nestled on the island tucked between the clear waters of the Caribbean Sea and the Atlantic Ocean, purchased a four-bedroom "dream house in a safe neighborhood" just a Texas leaguer or two away from the Atlantic Ocean in Santo Domingo, the capital city of the Dominican Republic. Framed against this backdrop, and with a live-in maid to boot, life was good for the Rodriguez clan.[2]

It nevertheless should be noted that life in the Dominican Republic was not such a Panglossian paradise for all of its inhabitants. The per capita gross national product (GNP) there as recently as 1995 was a mere

$1,438, compared to $27,550 in the United States. As a matter of fact, the average cat living in the United States consumed more beef than the average Central American. In addition, the life expectancy back then was roughly six years shorter for Dominicans than residents of the United States, and about 40 percent of Dominicans had no schooling. So, even with the advent of a new century, the plight of the Dominican Republic was rather drab—in direct contrast to the lush beauty of the island.[3]

Alex's initial interest in the game of baseball came from his father, himself a former professional catcher in the Dominican Republic. Moreover, it was in that country that Alex saw his first baseball games.

A natural born athlete, Rodriguez's free time was predictably packed with sports. Anyone searching for him could quickly spot him playing either in the street or in a park across the way from his house.

Because the Dominican Republic is hardly a rich nation, it follows that boys living there did not, as a rule, possess the finest equipment, nor did they play on the smoothest, finest diamonds. Rodriguez recalled, "In the [Dominican Republic], playing ball was tougher. No one had anything. In the United States there were $200 gloves, and the fields were like paradise."[4]

Often such poverty actually helped groom Dominican children as acrobatic fielders, playing on fields littered with pebbles. As former big-league shortstop Larry Bowa mentioned, on such infields a fielder was doomed to battle many a tough hop. As a result, though, such players learn to field their positions differently than American youngsters who play on better surfaces. It is a case of adaptation for the young players and of survival of the fittest for those who get good enough to leave the Latin American countries and make it in the majors.

Often, too, the children there improvised, devising their own variations of baseball. Alex, for example, loved playing a game his friends called "hot box," a variation of the American game run-down or pickle, and his favorite game of all was known as *platicka*.

That pastime involved taking old automobile license plates, bending them at a 90-degree angle, and using them as targets set up 90 feet from each other. Two pitchers would go up against two batters, attempting to knock down the plates with a rubber ball—somewhat like the aim of the sport of cricket. Furthermore, like cricket, the batters had to protect the "plate" by taking cuts at the ball with a makeshift bat.[5] In that respect, he was honing his skills much like New York children did when they took to their streets for a game of stickball.

In the Caribbean, baseball is seen as a passport "off the island" and from poverty to wealth, an opportunity to better oneself to "get a better standing," said Yankees reliever Mariano Rivera, a Panamanian. "In Latin countries, baseball is for the poor people." Plus, according to Bowa, those people often fill their time playing the game that they love (and thanks to the climate can play year-round) because they, unlike many youngsters in the United States, "still consider baseball their number-one sport." Plus that, the Dominican Republic is dotted with "many baseball academies"; it is clear that for many of the youngsters baseball is "their only chance."[6]

Of course, author Tim Wendel noted that budding stars from the Dominican Republic find "the route to the majors is a labyrinth; so arbitrary and Byzantine that one soon learns that the only hope is to play with joy. Revel in the moments and pray that the baseball gods look favorably upon the endeavor." He also quoted Pedro Martinez as saying of Dominicans' pulsating motivation, "All I know is that we need this game more than most people do."[7]

MIAMI BOUND

In any event, for the Rodriguez family, the good life on the island did not stay cozy for long; when Alex was eight years old the economy soured—his family reportedly lost their investment in their drug store after it had hemorrhaged cash month after month—and his folks were forced to sell their house, pack their belongings, and move to a small apartment in Miami, Florida. It was a trip of only a few hundred miles, but their destination was, figuratively, a world away. They told Alex they would soon return to the Dominican Republic, but that plan didn't transpire and Alex soon felt his parents had been dealt a tough blow in life.

In the classrooms of Miami, things were much more difficult for him than when he was on the playing fields of that city. In the fourth grade at Everglades Elementary School, he struggled with the English language. In his early days, living in Washington Heights, teeming with many Dominicans, he heard and spoke only Spanish. In the Dominican Republic, only Spanish was spoken, but in Miami, he would have to become bilingual. It took several years before he became comfortable with English.

In the meantime, young Alex came to idolize and emulate the baseball players he observed on television. If a favorite of his began to sport a black bat, Alex would apply shoe polish and a felt-tip pen to his own bat.[8] The one player he most admired was Cal Ripken Jr., the star shortstop—the position Alex wanted to play—of the Baltimore Orioles.[9]

Rodriguez had picked his role model wisely; traditionally, shortstops simply were not supposed to be tall men, but Ripken not only dispelled but also shattered the old baseball line labeling players, often shortstops, as "good glove, no stick."

Texas Rangers announcer Tom Grieve thinks the "no tall shortstops" concept was because, long ago, players "just weren't agile enough and didn't have the range to play shortstop." Now that is different due to, "The evolution of athletes in all sports. Players now are bigger, stronger, and quicker than they ever were before. Back then, the emphasis at shortstop was on defense, and very few shortstops hit for anything significant—there might have been some of them that hit .300, but very few had any kind of power to speak of." With men such as the 6' 4" Ripken, and later Rodriguez, the profile of shortstops has undergone a drastic redefining. "It's just incredible what's happened at the shortstop position," concluded Grieve.[10]

By the time Rodriguez was a freshman in high school, he already checked in with a 6' 1" frame, crammed with talent and tenacity; by then, the graceful Ripken Jr. had been an All-Star every year since 1983, forging the way for Rodriguez and a new generation of tall *and* potent shortstops.

Alex watched countless hours of major-league baseball games on cable television but viewed the game not only for sheer enjoyment but also with a trained eye, scrutinizing the hitters.[11]

Shortly after moving to Miami, Alex discovered a youth baseball team practicing at his school, so he would drop by and kibitz every day. Then, one lucky day, the team's coach, Juan Diego Arteaga, who needed a catcher, spotted Alex and asked him if he had ever caught before. Alex promptly lied, claiming to be a fine catcher, and, in fact, did well at that position despite playing with children several years older than he was.[12] Still, the competitive Rodriguez remembered that he was angry at times facing the more developed kids because he wasn't able to dominate in such situations.

Soon Alex developed a deep friendship with J. D., the son of his new coach, who, fortuitously, lived just two blocks from Alex. J. D. recalled the time his father called Rodriguez "the best player he'd ever seen. [Alex] was 11 years old. I thought, 'Crazy man, how can you say that?' But now look. I guess my dad was a pretty good scout."[13]

FATHER LEAVES, FATHER FIGURES ENTER

Alex's ups and downs continued; this time he was hit with a terrible emotional blow when his father abandoned the family. Shortly after Alex's ninth birthday, Victor told the family that he was leaving in order to make money for them, working for a short period of time in New York. He promised his children he would return. It was a lie. At first Alex angrily protested to his older sister, "Dad's coming back, you'll see," but after awhile his "hope dried up and died."[14] Many years later, he stated that the pain still gnawed at him.

He once simply muttered, "I couldn't understand what he had done."[15] Typical of adolescent thinking, he was shouldering a huge but self-imposed burden. Years after the fact, he reiterated, "To this day, I still don't really know how a man could do that to his family, to turn his back."[16] Baffled, Alex would gain little solace from the rare phone calls Victor eventually did make to his son.

Alex finally reached the point at which he said, "All the love I had for him I just gave to my mother."[17] Ultimately his parents were divorced, an uneasy issue that Alex had to deal with.

The mystery of the vanishing father later was explained to Alex by his mother. "I found out that Miami wasn't fast-paced enough for Dad," began Alex, "that he wanted to go back to New York and Mom didn't. They talked but couldn't agree. So, he split."[18]

Many kids in Alex's situation would have become introverted and diffident. Rich Hofman, who coached Alex in high school, said Alex dealt with his split with his father so well partly because "he's got this unique ability to say the right things at the right time all the time. I'm sure he's got his moments, but he's very private and you're not going to see those moments. Maybe only his wife does." On the outside, though, even back in high school, Hofman said Alex was "always poised."[19]

Six months of financial struggles followed Victor's departure from Miami, but Lourdes, who held down several jobs, working in a Miami immigration office during the day and working as a waitress for two restaurants, eked out a sufficient living. Later she would start her own immigration office, helping fellow Dominicans adjust to life in the United States and guiding them to become legal residents and even citizens. She later would own a restaurant as well; in this family, ambition and ability were not unique to her destined-to-be-famous son Alex. She frequently reassured her children that things somehow would be fine, just as on the eve of her son's first big-league game she calmly told him, "You were born to be one [a ballplayer]. You will be fine."[20]

Additionally, Lourdes, Susy, who would go on to earn a law degree, Joe, who later went into business, and other relatives lavished their love on Alex. Juan Arteaga continued to play an enormous role in Alex's life; eventually Alex considered him to be his second father. As Rodriguez put it, "He was the father I didn't have. Everything he gave to his son, he gave to me."[21] Alex appreciated that Arteaga had guided him, provided for him, and had, in short, taken care of him.

Arteaga, for instance, introduced seven-year-old Alex to the Boys and Girls Club of Miami, where Eddie Rodriguez, no relation to Alex, also would become a father figure. Eddie recalled, "I was his mentor, with him through the good and the bad."[22]

Eddie not only ran programs and coached baseball there, but, as a former minor-league player, he kindled a desire in Alex to play professional baseball. Plus, having coached Jose Canseco, Rafael Palmeiro, Danny Tartabull, and Alex Fernandez at the Boys Club, Eddie knew, and shared with young Alex, tales of those who had preceded him and made it to the majors. Eddie was quick to give Alex advice about believing in himself while also demanding more from himself. Such a philosophy, Eddie asserted, would get one through both the good times as well as the bad ones.

At that time, Lourdes could not afford the fee required to register Alex to play with the Boys Club, but Arteaga arranged for the boy to play and to be sufficiently equipped to take the field, generously buying him baseball equipment.

Alex later would write that even though he was "shy and skinny," he made good, winning the city league's batting crown, his first such title, and he helped his team win three city championships as well.[23] Normally, he manned the shortstop position, but when J. D Arteaga took to the hill, Alex would hunker down behind home plate as the catcher, just as he had the first time he played for J. D.'s father.

His mother and older siblings were usually too busy earning cash for the household to attend his games. Also, the other children on the team could afford snacks, which their parents provided, say, between games of doubleheaders. All this hurt Alex and made him feel "like an underdog," but he somehow managed to stay buoyant.[24]

"After a while, I lied to myself," Rodriguez said. "I tried to tell myself that it [his father's absence and its ramifications] didn't matter, that I didn't care. But times I was alone, I often cried. Where was my father?"[25]

His brother, Joe, found time to play baseball with Alex and taught him a tough yet valuable lesson. As Alex put it, "He pitched to me in our games and he'd always let me win—until the end of the game."[26] At that point, Joe would pour it on and take victory from Alex, which prompted Alex to crave improvement.

Perhaps the string of victories Alex's teams ran up helped salve his feelings as he helped lead his team to two national championships and three city titles. Eddie Rodriguez recalled there would be times when Alex was about 10 when "we'd look for Alex on the on-deck circle and where's he at—he's playing basketball [nearby]. We'd have to chase him. He was always on the go."[27]

At one point, over a four-year stretch, Alex attended four different schools and even, as a seventh-grade student at Kendall Academy, was deft enough to play baseball on the varsity team, obviously competing against young men as much as five years older and more experienced than himself.

HIGH SCHOOL DAYS BEGIN

When he was a freshman at Christopher Columbus Catholic High School, he made the varsity basketball team and did well on the court, often as the starting point guard (in 1997, his love for the round ball still intact, he worked out with the NBA's Seattle SuperSonics and did not embarrass himself; their coach complimented him on his quick feet and hands). Rodriguez was the only freshman to ever start in the school's history; he was 6'1" and possessed quickness, vital in all sports. Later, he even received basketball offers from Stetson University, the University of Mississippi, and Florida State University.

Eventually, in order to balance sports and education, his mother insisted Alex sign up for only two sports. He would opt for baseball, saying it was "in my blood," and for football, as the tail end of the hoop season conflicted with early spring baseball. Also, giving up basketball freed him to devote more prep work for baseball.[28]

However, his high school baseball coach informed Alex that he probably would languish on the bench as the backup shortstop for the following two seasons. He even suggested Rodriguez would have to wait until his senior year to see much action at all.

Faced with such a plight, Rodriguez made two decisions: (1) He would work harder than he had in the past, and (2) he would take the advice of Juan Arteaga and his son and join J. D. at Miami's Westminster Christian High School, a private school and a baseball factory despite an enrollment of only about 200 to 300 students, for his sophomore year.[29]

Lourdes found Westminster's religious curriculum and the school's demands for respect and responsibility especially attractive for her son.[30]

Still, the lofty tuition of $5,000 presented a problem for the Rodriguez clan. Juan Arteaga stepped in and solved the issue, convincing the Westminster Christian coach to give him a look. Shortly after that took place, financial aid was arranged and Alex was enrolled at the school.

It did not take long for Alex to establish his popularity. "He had a quick smile and never acted like a big shot. And the girls liked the handsome new boy with the green eyes." He gained the nickname "Cheech," based on a Latin American comedian, but related to people of all races.[31]

Bill Henderson, who coached at Westminster Christian and was their athletic director, recalled Alex as respectful but not shy. "He had a degree of respect for his elders that I think parents hope their kids have. And his quality of asking questions is a real good one and requires a degree of boldness to be able to do that. He played with a lot of poise for sure, and he always wanted to do the right thing regardless of whether it was on the field or off the field."[32]

In the hallways of the school Alex came off as "more than just one of the guys; he was a pretty popular guy, a good-looking guy, tall and [athletic], but certainly nobody knew he was going to be A-Rod." Henderson saw Rodriguez as more of a reserved star than the stereotypical BMOC.[33]

For Alex, blessed with the nearly tropical weather of southern Florida, baseball was ubiquitous. A typical day as a Westminster Warrior, both long and arduous, however, was more than just baseball. For one thing, beyond the demands of the classroom, attending his new school required a car drive of approximately a half-hour, forcing Rodriguez to wake up extremely early in order to leave the house daily at 6:30 A.M. He did not return home until 8:00 P.M.[34]

The grind notwithstanding, Alex did what he has done throughout his life: He achieved. It took some time, but he went on to make the honor roll, a feat he is still proud of. Even when he was somewhat caught up in the hoopla of his senior year, he stated, "My level of play didn't drop and I stayed on top of my grades."[35]

Tragedy struck that year when, during the middle of a Westminster Christian football game, Juan Arteaga collapsed in the bleachers. A helicopter was dispatched to the school, where it landed on the football field and then whisked Arteaga to a hospital. Arteaga, who had a history of heart problems, died later that day, prompting Rodriguez to say he felt as if "someone had torn my heart out and smashed it."[36]

Having played the glamour positions of quarterback—he would go on to be *Parade* magazine's all-American QB selection after his junior season—and then point guard on the basketball team, it was spring and time for baseball. He struggled at the plate as a sophomore, hitting a paltry .256, the lowest batting average he ever had hit and, for that matter, the lowest he ever would hit at any level in a season with 150 or more at bats. He attributed his season-long slumber to having just experienced a growth spurt. Despite his 6' 3", 195-pound frame, his arm remained un-impressive, and he barely managed to hit the 200-pound plateau while bench-pressing. By his senior year, he could bench about 325 pounds.

At that time, Hofman had coached about 125 players (now up to more than 200) who went on to play college ball and 20 who advanced to pro ball (that total is now up to about 35) and had built the school's baseball program from scratch, swiftly elevating them into a powerhouse. Through 2006, Hofman, now at Piper High School in the Fort Lauderdale area, owned 937 victories and had won 10 state championships, 8 at Westmin-ster Christian, including two national titles in 1992 and 1996.

In 1992, Rodriguez's junior year, of the nine regulars Hofman employed, seven would go on to play pro ball, including four future major leaguers. "I had Alex at short," Hofman recalled, "Mickey Lopez was at second base, Doug Mientkiewicz was our catcher, and Dan Perkins [a second-round pro pick] was a pitcher and third baseman. And J. D. [Arteaga] went to Triple-A, probably would have been called up but he had a decision to make," and opted to take a coaching job at the University of Miami.[37]

"When he was a sophomore, Alex had some holes in his swing and he was a little undisciplined offensively—he didn't even hit .300 then, but that summer he really worked hard." He heeded Hofman's advice to become more patient and to take cuts at pitches he could handle rather than hitting what is known as pitchers' pitches. Before, he had been essentially striking himself out. Having patience helped fix this. "He started doing that and he never looked back. I predicted greatness for him. I felt he would be a great player, but I can't really say that [I knew] he was going to be in the Hall of Fame someday." Nor, he said, did he envision Rodriguez hitting for such power, "but I felt he could win a bat-ting championship."[38]

Hofman encouraged Rodriguez, saying he was satisfied with Alex's early showing and predicting that by the end of his junior season, "everyone will get to know you, and in 12th grade you'll be the number one pick in the country." Buoyed by his coach's faith in him, Rodriguez continued his regimen, vowing to improve.[39] Later Rodriguez would comment, "Coach Hofman was more than just a coach—he was a mentor, teacher, and a counselor."[40]

Meanwhile, Bill Henderson recalled that when Alex was a sophomore and junior, "It was debatable whether he was the best guy on the team. I can tell you with a lot of confidence there's probably never been a better high school baseball team in the history of this country when Alex was a junior." The players who did not go on to play pro ball, "the guys filling in the gaps still went off to college and played. Being around such other good players humbled him."[41]

AMAZING JUNIOR AND SENIOR YEARS

By the time Rodriguez entered his junior year, he was benching a fantastic 300–310 pounds and was launching 400-foot drives, at times over the left-field fence of his home diamond and into a swimming pool that sat a bit beyond the barrier. He called such blows "pool shots" and was depositing balls there long before major leaguers drove home runs into the luxurious pool at Arizona's Bank One Ballpark.

Hofman recalled Alex as being "tall and skinny, but he went from around 155 pounds to around 180 between his sophomore and junior year, then up around another 10 pounds by his senior year. The scouts didn't even recognize him between his sophomore and junior year."[42] Yet as a sophomore he was not a very strong kid, nor was he a polished hitter.

Hofman stated Alex had a tendency to swing "at borderline pitches, often first pitches, and pitchers' pitches rather than balls that he could drive." Then, in the summer after his sophomore season, listening to Hofman's advise about being more selective, his average shot up and the starting shortstop job was now firmly his.[43]

Like so many players who evolve into major-league stars, Rodriguez put up monstrous numbers in high school. Playing for Westminster Christian, he helped lead them to a national championship, as selected by both the National High School Baseball Coaches Association and the prestigious *Baseball America* in 1992, his junior year. His statistics glistened: He hit .477 with 51 runs scored, cracked out six home runs, recorded an on-base percentage nearing .600, and stole 42 bases as the team went 33–2. The Warriors won the state AA championship behind their leadoff hitting star Rodriguez; their number three hitter, future big leaguer Doug Mientkiewicz; J. D. Arteaga, who tossed a five-hit shutout in the title game; Steve Butler, an all-American hurler; and a nice supporting cast behind them.[44]

It had been an especially rewarding year for Rodriguez, especially considering that by season's end opposing teams, fearing his stick, fed him a fastball-free diet of pitches. Often he would nurse a walk, however, and convert that into a double via a stolen base, meaning the enemy was damned if they did—pitch to him—and damned if they didn't.

During summer 1992, he joined the USA Junior National Team and traveled to play in Monterrey, Mexico, competing against the top 17- and

18-year-olds from far and wide. There, he tied teammate Jerrod Wong for the most home runs, six, while also leading the U.S. team with a blistering 16 RBIs in just 13 games. He had the chore of beating out a trio of talented shortstops, but he did so, going on to hit .425 while playing the field in every inning of every game. His team, opposing a globe of talent, managed a laudatory second-place finish in the World Junior Championships.

It was while playing in the championship that he learned of the devastation leveled by Hurricane Andrew as it pounded into Miami with its mighty 190-mile-an-hour winds, claiming the lives of 32 and causing $3 billion worth of havoc. It took three days before he was able to reach his family to learn they were all well. His school was so badly battered, the start of his senior year was put on hold for six weeks, and briefly there was talk that all sports would be wiped out.[45]

After the sports programs were up and running, Rodriguez, who was on his way to his second selection as an all-state quarterback, broke several school passing marks. Rich Hofman recalled, furthermore, that Alex "had no line to protect him his senior year. He'd get back to set up to throw and they'd [the defense] be greeting him when he got there. He went down under a punt, he was the 'force' guy, now called 'gunners,' the outside man who's supposed to cover the punt, and he dove to try to tackle a punt returner and his wrist got injured, so he stopped playing the rest of the year. There were a couple of scouts there watching, and they were horrified." Fortunately, the injury proved to be a mere hairline fracture.[46]

His senior season was also the year he decided to forsake a sport he loved, basketball, to devote all of his energy to baseball. Before the baseball season opened, he and his closest friend, J. D. Arteaga, signed letters of intent to play on the diamonds of the University of Miami. Alex was considering the study of law or medicine just in case his baseball career somehow did not pan out.[47]

At Westminster Christian, he nearly helped take the team to back-to-back state titles in baseball, thwarted only by a defeat to West Palm Beach Cardinal Newman, Alex's final high school game, one which Coach Rich Hofman spoke of as a way "to show his greatness and even his vulnerability. It shows the highs and the lows in somebody's career, and he's had many, many highs. We were playing in the regional playoff game and it came down to the last out. Our ninth hitter reached on a little dribbler down the third base line. We were down by one run and I said, 'Please, just let us get to Alex.' Alex came up and it was our last out. He hit a tremendous shot in the top of the seventh; it cleared the fence by about 40 feet in right center field, it hit an orchard out there. The center fielder did a smart thing, he came running in holding up his hands like it bounced over and the umpire bought it—he called a ground rule double. Alex and I both should have been thrown out of the game because we were just screaming at the umpire. We did score two runs and took the lead, but they tied it.

"In the bottom of the ninth inning, Alex had a double-play ball that he threw past the second baseman and they won the game. He committed three errors in that ballgame; he still talks about it some today. I said to him, 'Man, you've done so many things for us over the years.' I couldn't even feel bad about that." It was regrettable that the team, number one ranked in the country, fell three wins shy of winning the state title. "It was the only year out of the '90's that I didn't go to the state final four."[48]

Overall, the Warriors posted a sparkling 28–5 win-loss ledger, but Alex said he would never forget his misplay. It remained, he said, a motivating factor to never assume anything is a fait accompli. His coach called the play one Alex normally handled routinely, and he stressed that, after all his star had done for the team, he was not about to start blaming him. He had, on his final high school fielding chance, committed the most humbling error of his young career.

For his toil in his senior year, Rodriguez was named a first-team prep all-American, thanks largely to his gaudy .505 batting average, going 47 for 93. Over one particularly scorching stretch of games, he reached base safely 21 times as pitchers found him to be virtually omnipresent on the base paths; for the year his on-base percentage was an ungodly .712.

His power numbers gleamed, too, with nine home runs and 36 RBIs over his 33-game schedule. Further, he averaged better than one stolen base per game played, flawlessly swiping 35 bases in 35 tries. It got to the point at which local newspapers covered his exploits with the intensity and scope usually reserved for one of celebrity status. They even dubbed him with the heady, laudatory nickname "Superman."[49]

The Man of Steel metaphor was fitting: his eyesight was as keen as supervision, he flew on the base paths with bulletlike speed, and he possessed unlimited power. His only shortcoming was his inability to leap tall buildings in a single bound.

In his final two years in high school, Rodriguez was their catalyst as the leadoff hitter—but one with power—Hofman, said he hit "around six home runs in six consecutive games at the beginning of his senior season—but as a sophomore he probably hit sixth or seventh. We were always in the national limelight, and he had good players around him so you couldn't walk him every time. As a junior, he was the star, but we had Doug [Mientkiewicz] and Mickey [Lopez], too. They were our senior leaders, so Alex didn't have to carry the team by himself."[50]

SCOUTS' SCRUTINY, BIG-LEAGUE DESTINY

With Rodriguez's ability and potential, it had been little wonder that a reported 68 scouts, 6 of them from the salivating Seattle Mariners, who would own the first pick in the upcoming draft, had inundated the ballpark to see his first game as a senior—Rodriguez routinely homered and tossed in two other hits that day—and their numbers swelled to more than 70 for the next contest, a three-for-four showing with a homer tossed in.[51]

One account has the scouts, armed with radar guns and stopwatches, at the season opener representing about two-thirds of the total attendance of approximately one hundred. That same source also indicates crowds topping the 1,000 mark became the norm that year and youngsters coming out to beg Rodriguez for his autograph.[52]

One of the scouts opined, "He's the next Cal Ripken. He's not just a field-and-throw guy, he's got all of the tools." In addition, after Ripken first had seen Rodriguez in person, he sang his praise and commented that their styles were quite similar. He went as far as to say that if Alex someday joined his Orioles, he would gladly switch from his shortstop position to third to make way for Rodriguez. Ironically, it later would be Rodriguez who would move to third base, first for Ripken, later for Derek Jeter.[53]

Clearly, by now, everyone knew of Alex, the rising star. To help Alex out, his sister Susy fielded the flood of phone calls that inevitably came, as many as forty on a given night from agents, from scouts, and from college coaches and recruiters.[54]

Incidentally, one report has a remarkable 30 pro scouts popping by the school to check out Rodriguez's first scrimmage, and the Mariners instructed two of their scouts to tag along with Rodriguez throughout his entire senior year.[55]

Such under-the-microscope pressure, which began for Alex as early as the age of 14, was at times "overwhelming." He commented, "Growing up, it's like there was a label on my head." Furthermore, with all the hype came the chance for complacency to set in, but Rodriguez "never wanted that to happen to me. I used the label to make myself work harder."[56]

His glittering senior stats earned him honors as the USA Baseball Junior Player of the Year and Gatorade's National Student Athlete of the Year, honors won just one year earlier by his friend Derek Jeter.

Although he did not capture the Golden Spikes Award, which is given yearly to the best amateur player in the nation, he was tabbed as one of the finalists. That honor went to another future major leaguer, Darren Dreifort, who already was playing college ball at Wichita State University.

Rodriguez was only the second high school ballplayer ever to be a finalist for the illustrious award; the other was Ken Griffey Jr., soon to be a teammate of Rodriguez.

For his three-year Westminster career, he compiled 124 hits good for a lofty .419 average, swatted 17 homers, drove in 70 runs in 100 contests, and, as a catalyst, tossed in 135 runs scored and 90 stolen bases out of 94 attempts. He was a true winner, with his team sporting a win-loss percentage of .870.

In February 1993, the World Trade Center was bombed and five people perished. In baseball, a 70-year-old Minnie Minoso appeared in a minor-league game.

It was also the year that Rodriguez was thrilled when he made a visit to the Baltimore Orioles spring training camp in Fort Lauderdale, Florida. It was there that he first met his baseball role model, Cal Ripken Jr. Ripken observed, "My first impression was that he was physically mature. I assumed he'd be a little meek and underdeveloped."[57]

When the 1993 June draft rolled around, the Mariners gobbled him up, ignoring the more seasoned Dreifort, a shrewd move as Dreifort posted a lifetime 48–60 record. As the first player selected overall in the draft, he joined such big names from the past as Chipper Jones and Griffey Jr.

The phone call that came from the Mariners on June 3, 1993, giving Rodriguez the news, delighted his friends and family who had expectantly clustered around him that day on the Arteaga family's patio. Alex confided that he was delighted to be the first pick and recognized the inherent challenge.

The party was crashed, so to speak, when Alex's long-departed father called him "out of the blue." The phone call "shocked Alex" while making Lourdes upset and livid. Alex explained that his mother wanted the day to be special for Alex and that she felt that his dad had absolutely "no right to be a part of it." There was no immediate follow-up to the conversation; the two were once again incommunicado.[58]

Rodriguez, although pleased, was also hesitant to sign with Seattle, a team that hardly had a winning reputation, unlike Rodriguez, who was accustomed to winning, having won eight championships over his previous 10 years in baseball. He also realized that Seattle, an American League club, would not visit the Miami vicinity. Interleague play was still four years in the future, and even then. during the first five years, interleague play consisted solely of teams playing against others from the same division in the other league, meaning that Rodriguez might never play before a hometown crowd in Miami.

On the eve of the draft, Seattle's vice president for scouting and player development, Roger Jongewaard, called Alex to inform him that he almost assuredly was going to be their first selection. Rodriguez pleaded that Jongewaard reconsider. The Mariners' scouts coveted him, and Jongewaard praised his strong arm, calling it "double plus. Two grades above the major league average."[59] Clearly, Seattle was not going to pass up the chance to snag this talent.

Just because they drafted him did not mean he had to sign with them. Already, Rodriguez had built up an eye-catching résumé. He realized that if he did not sign to play pro ball, he simply could play for the Miami Hurricanes, wait a year, and reenter major-league baseball's draft. Barring a freakish occurrence, another club other than the Mariners assuredly would draft him then.

Rodriguez had another advantage because he had taken on the high-profile Scott Boras as his agent. Boras was a man known for his hard-nosed approach and for his ability to squeeze piles of dollars out of teams. He had spent four years in the minor leagues. Then, hindered by three injuries, he retired and soon became an impact player, using his briefcase and savvy rather than a glove and bat.

Just a few years before taking on Rodriguez as a client, Boras had negotiated, employing his customary hardball tactics, the contract of 18-year-old pitcher Brien Taylor, the overall first pick in the draft. After negotiations dragged on until the day before the Yankees would have lost Taylor to a college, he signed an inflated contract for $1.55 million. He lingered in the low minors and wound up becoming only the second player ever to be the number one draft selection never to make it to the majors.[60] Boras "had a reputation for taking negotiations right to the brink," so when negotiations between Boras and the Mariners became laborious and lengthy (and later, lucrative), it was hardly shocking.[61]

In the meantime, Rodriguez's ability and budding fame were so great, he became the first high school baseball player ever, and just one of 19 young players that year, to be invited to the tryouts for Team USA, doing so in 1993. He was on a roll.

First came an important lesson, however, one he labeled his "first taste of the business side of baseball." A company, Topps, that produced baseball cards was the sponsor for Team USA, and they wanted each of the players to be included in one of their card sets. Rodriguez learned that move would hurt him to the tune of $500,000 "in lost income with another baseball company" that wanted the rights to print the very first Alex Rodriguez card, destined, they believed, to be a classic for collectors.[62]

Refusing to sign a deal with the card company resulted in his being compelled to leave the squad, missing out on a world tour. The Team USA coach, John Anderson, was upset at the loss of Rodriguez, describing him as "a 17 year old with a 25 year old body."[63]

Soon after, as a member of the Junior National's South team at the U.S. Olympic Festival in San Antonio, Texas, he went four for eight before his luck tapered off on July 28. It was then that Rodriguez was lounging in the dugout when a wild pregame warm-up throw from the opposing second baseman smacked his right cheek, resulting in a broken cheekbone.

The injury was serious enough to require cosmetic surgery three days later on August 1. He later wrote that his "caved-in face" was repaired much like an auto body worker repairs a car's dent: The surgeon "inserted a rod that popped my cheekbone back to normal." As ugly as that procedure sounds, he was fortunate; if the ball's impact had struck one inch higher, death could have resulted; one inch to the side, and the loss of an eye easily could have occurred.[64] Even after being repaired, he refused to pick up a baseball for about ten weeks.[65] As a further precaution, he insured himself with Lloyd's of London for $1 million.[66]

The drooling Mariners desperately wanted to ink Rodriguez to a contract. It would not be all that easy. It took until August 31 to persuade him to sign, just hours before he would have packed his belongings and plodded off to the University of Miami campus, leaving the Mariners empty-handed; once he attended a class in college, they would forfeit their right to sign him.

Seattle scout Fernando Arguelles finally signed him to a three-year pact that enabled Rodriguez to earn $1.3 million through 1996. Boras felt he could have held out for a heftier signing bonus, but Rodriguez, anxious to play the game he treasured, signed.[67]

A clause in the contract also assured Rodriguez he would be called up to the major leagues when rosters expanded beyond the norm of 25 men in September. As it turned out, the Mariners would beckon for him in less than a year.

He suddenly felt as rich as James Earl Jones's magnificent voice, but, not one to splurge on himself, Rodriguez's only indulgence was the purchase of a Jeep Cherokee. He also "forced himself not to spend more than $1,000 per month. Before long, those dollar amounts would look like pocket change."[68] In fact, the $1,000 per month allotment amounted to "less than the minimum minor league salary." His sole expenditures of any excess was the purchase of a new Mercedes-Benz for his mother and the paying off of her mortgage; she was able to retire, worry free at last.[69]

Pecuniary matters behind him, an elated Rodriguez anxiously awaited his first spring as a professional ballplayer.

Almost seven-and-a-half years later, reflecting on this period in his life, Rodriguez commented, "I've always said the happiest I've ever been is when the Mariners signed me and gave me my first million dollars. At 17 years old, I thought that was pretty scary."[70]

NOTES

1. Tim Wendel, *The New Face of Baseball: The 100-Year Rise and Triumph of Latinos in America's Favorite Sport* (New York: HarperCollins, 2003), 181.

2. Alex Rodriguez and Greg Brown, *Hit a Grand Slam* (Dallas: Taylor, 1998), 8–9.

3. Marcelo M. Suárez-Orozco and Mariela M. Páez, eds., *Latinos Remaking America* (Berkeley and Los Angeles: University of California Press, 2002), 23–24.

4. Michael A. Pare, *Sports Stars, Series 3* (Detroit: UXL, 1970), 241.

5. Rodriguez and Brown, *Hit a Grand Slam,* 10.

6. Wendel, *The New Face of Baseball,* 51, 80, 186.

7. Ibid., 179–80.

8. Ibid., 12.

9. Marylou Morano Kjelle, *Alex Rodriguez: Professional Baseball Player* (Hockessin, DE: Mitchell Lane, 2006), 15.

10. Author's interview with Tom Grieve, March 8, 2006.

11. Stew Thornley, *Alex Rodriguez: Slugging Shortstop* (Minneapolis, MN: Lerner, 1998), 16.

12. Rodriguez and Brown, *Hit a Grand Slam,* 13.

13. Jim Gallagher, *Alex Rodriguez: Latinos in Baseball* (Childs, MD: Mitchell Lane, 2000), 14.

14. Rodriguez and Brown, *Hit a Grand Slam,* 14.

15. Mike Shalin, *Alex Rodriguez: A + Shortstop* (Champaign, IL: Sports Publishing, 1999), 16.

16. Steve Riach, *Heart of a Champion: Profiles in Character,* with John Humphrey (Nashville, TN: Broadman and Holman, 2001), 16.

17. Pare, *Sports Stars,* 241.

18. Shalin, *Alex Rodriguez: A + Shortstop,* 16.

19. Author's interview with Rich Hofman, May 3, 2006.

20. Gallagher, *Alex Rodriguez: Latinos in Baseball,* 25.

21. Thornley, *Alex Rodriguez: Slugging Shortstop,* 17.

22. Author's interview with Eddie Rodriguez, July 6, 2006.

23. Rodriguez and Brown, *Hit a Grand Slam,* 18.

24. Rodriguez and Brown, *Hit a Grand Slam,* 18.

25. Riach, *Heart of a Champion,* 17.

26. Ken Rappoport, *Super Sports Star Alex Rodriguez* (Berkeley Heights, NJ: Enslow, 2004), 12.

27. Author's interview with Eddie Rodriguez, July 6, 2006.

28. Ibid., 25, 27.

29. Rodriguez and Brown, *Hit a Grand Slam,* 22–23.

30. Stout, *On the Field With . . . Alex Rodriguez*, 19.

31. Ibid., 23.

32. Author's interview with Bill Henderson, July 2006.

33. Ibid.

34. Rodriguez and Brown, *Hit a Grand Slam*, 24.

35. Stewart, *Alex Rodriguez: Gunning for Greatness*, 13.

36. Rodriguez and Brown, *Hit a Grand Slam*, 25.

37. Author's interview with Rich Hofman, May 3, 2006.

38. Ibid.

39. Rodriguez and Brown, *Hit a Grand Slam*, 24.

40. Alex Rodriguez, "Arod's Journal," *AROD: The Official Site of Alex Rodriguez* (April 3, 2006), available at http://arod.mlb.com/players/rodriguez_alex/journal.jsp#april3.

41. Author's interview with Bill Henderson, July 2006.

42. Author's interview with Rich Hofman, May 3, 2006.

43. Ibid.

44. Stewart, *Alex Rodriguez: Gunning for Greatness*, 14–15; Stout, *On the Field With . . . Alex Rodriguez*, 31.

45. Rodriguez and Brown, *Hit a Grand Slam*, 27.

46. Author's interview with Rich Hofman, May 3, 2006.

47. Macnow, *Sports Great, Alex Rodriguez*, 24.

48. Author's interview with Rich Hofman, May 3, 2006.

49. Stewart, *Alex Rodriguez: Gunning for Greatness*, 17–18.

50. Author's interview with Rich Hofman, May 3, 2006.

51. Rodriguez and Brown, *Hit a Grand Slam*, 28.

52. Stout, *On the Field With . . . Alex Rodriguez*, 36, 38.

53. Macnow, *Sports Great, Alex Rodriguez*, 26, 28.

54. Rodriguez and Brown, *Hit a Grand Slam*, 28.

55. Stewart, *Alex Rodriguez: Gunning for Greatness*, 16.

56. John Hickey, "Alex Rodriguez Not a Typical Superstar," *Baseball Digest*, July 2000, 42.

57. Rappoport, *Super Sports Star Alex Rodriguez*, 15.

58. Shalin, *Alex Rodriguez: A + Shortstop*, 17.

59. Thornley, *Alex Rodriguez: Slugging Shortstop*, 30.

60. "Brien Taylor," *Wikipedia: The Free Encyclopedia* (February 2007), available at http://en.wikipedia.org/wiki/Brien_Taylor.

61. Stewart, *Alex Rodriguez: Gunning for Greatness*, 19.

62. Rodriguez and Brown, *Hit a Grand Slam*, 29.

63. Stewart, *Alex Rodriguez: Gunning for Greatness*, 20.

64. Rodriguez and Brown, *Hit a Grand Slam*, 29.

65. Macnow, *Sports Great, Alex Rodriguez*, 31.

66. Stewart, *Alex Rodriguez: Gunning for Greatness*, 21.

67. Steven Goldman, ed., *Mind Game: How the Boston Red Sox Got Smart, Won a World Series, and Created a New Blueprint for Winning* (New York: Workman, 2005), 181.

68. Christensen, *Alex Rodriguez*, 17.

69. Stout, *On the Field With . . . Alex Rodriguez*, 57.

70. Covert, *Alex Rodriguez*, 16.

Chapter 2

PERSONALITY OF THE MAN

Those who contend adults' basic personalities are shaped at a very early age need look no farther than Alex Rodriguez for verification of that theory. His mother said that he was "focused" from childhood on, almost monomaniacal in his interest in baseball. "He didn't care about the sun or the rain. He just had to play ball." He even would weep if his mother did not take him to a nearby park.[1] Even in high school, he was so intent on baseball he did not attend the prom or homecoming events.

Rodriguez's high school baseball coach, Rich Hofman, recalled that Alex "was kind of like a sponge, he absorbed everything. He enjoyed life. The school embraced him. He was just one of the guys, he hung out with the guys. He's not one of the guys you have 1,000 stories about and everybody laughs. Alex was the kind of guy who always enjoyed himself, but he would never *do* the jokes, he'd always suggest it to somebody else and then they'd get in trouble and he'd just laugh and kind of be in the background. He was a practical joker, but you could never catch him at anything—he'd always put somebody else up to it." If he ever did get caught, "he'd just kind of smile."[2]

Eddie Rodriguez, now a unit director with the Boys and Girls Club in Miami, said Alex, with whom he speaks almost daily, is the type of person who tries to do everything right all the time, a perfectionist. "He always tries to do what's best for everybody." Eddie said he feels Alex has a "good, clean image" and wants to maintain it. "He's in the eyes of the public; if he makes one wrong move, one mistake, his reputation can come down."[3]

Dr. Claudia Springer recalled, "I had him in a Bible class, and he was a diligent, competent student. The only anecdote I have is that he and his good friend, J. D. Arteaga, once played a rather ingenious prank on me while I had a classroom full of his classmates. The old doors to the room had an arm extending outside the doorframe at the top that kept the door from slamming shut, a sort of pneumatic closing mechanism. One day he and J. D., both of whom are very tall and would have been about the only ones who could have pulled this off, waited until my class was full of students, then tied a T shirt around the arm, keeping the two parts of it from separating and forcing the door to remain closed. They had been absolutely silent, so I had no idea they were there until they knocked on the door and ran. I had to call the office on the room intercom to get the maintenance head to come let us all out. When we saw it was a baseball jersey and heard giggling down the hall, we glanced up to see the two boys watching the process from the corner."[4]

Hofman picked up his take on Alex. "He worked hard; out of all the guys there he probably, from a material standpoint, probably ranked in the lower part of the group, but they were all kind of considered equal at the school—he was never looked down upon. He was always very outgoing and positive. He was fun to have around. He was just a normal kid whose mother worked really hard and he didn't have a lot of money but he never seemed like there was a problem, he was just a normal kid who fit in well with his environment.

"Alex is a private person and you, in order to have real personal, intimate conversations, you have to have a lot of contact. We don't get a chance to do that as much as I would like, but I understand. He knows that I'm always here for him and I think if I needed something he would be there for me.

"He has a very small inner circle, by design. When you get to be a star of his magnitude there are a lot of reasons why people want to be friends with you, so you have to be very leery of that." Those in that circle are treated well. "Not many high school coaches get to have the experiences that I've had because I've had a player of Alex's extraordinary talents. I've gone to All-Star games and been able to get preferential treatment from people in the clubhouses and been able to go places where most coaches can't go."[5]

Tom Grieve, a former outfielder, feels Rodriguez is "a very competent person, so in that regard I'd say he's outgoing." Like many players, A-Rod tends to be "more comfortable among his friends in a clubhouse environment. He's also a guy, maybe unlike many ballplayers, who's very comfortable in a corporate setting, in a business suit in a business environment at a Fortune 500 company. He's a very savvy person when it comes to business. He's got a lot of money, and I think he takes pride in the fact that he's not just delegating that authority to other people. I think he plays a major role in everything that goes on in his life. I'm impressed by that."[6]

Eddie Rodriguez observed, "I think he's at the point [at which] he knows who's going to be in his corner. What people don't remember is Alex's been a superstar since he was 15 years old; at 20-something years old he made $250 million. People don't realize that you can have [millions of dollars] and you get sick and you have problems just like a guy that makes two cents an hour, but people portray it like athletes are perfect—like you're a robot, you can't get sick, or can't miss a ground ball, or you can't strike out, and that's totally wrong." Sometimes, said Eddie, having millions "can be dangerous" and can lead to criticism such as "You don't hit with men in scoring position, you choke." However, Eddie said that aside from nitpicking, "They cannot say that he's not a good person."[7]

Meanwhile, Bill Henderson chipped in, "Alex has a sort of built-in sensitivity for who he gets close to and people he enjoys being with now— if he had a connection from the past when he was, quote, nothing, not yet A-Rod, when he was just Alex Rodriguez—there's automatically a degree of comfort that is there. I'm six years older than he is. When I was coaching him I was 24 and he was 18, 24 might as well be 44 at that age. That gap is a big deal. Rich Hofman was more of a father figure, I think I was like an uncle. At this point that six-year age gap, especially with the life that he's led—he's matured quickly—I think that respect and comfort is very much there [with us], but we now speak and evaluate and discuss things on a very even level."[8]

PRIDE, DEVOTION, AND GENEROSITY

Hofman stated he is most proud of Rodriguez for the way "he matured as a young man and became a father and a husband; and his terrific work ethic and how he approaches the game, just the individual stuff as a person [not as a superstar]." On the other hand, he noted, "Just like every other fan in America, I'm in awe of the fact that I was able to coach probably one of the greatest players of all time. The most important thing to me is the type of the relationship and the admiration that we have for each other and I guard that a lot. Then there's the part of me that's a baseball fan that thinks just as much of him as other people do. I don't idolize him but I really take a lot of pride in the fact that I was his high school coach and he acknowledges me as his coach."[9]

Rodriguez truly is devoted to his mother, Lourdes, and was said to have called her from Seattle almost daily. In the dedication to his 1998 book *Hit a Grand Slam*, he wrote that the book was for his mother, who instilled in him "family values through her daily examples of love, courage, dedication, and sacrifice." Even back then he was aware of how baseball stars attract phonies and sycophants, so he singled out his family for their unconditional love and support. The generous Rodriguez also donated his proceeds from his book to the Boys and Girls Clubs of America.[10]

Coincidentally, the executive director of the Boys and Girls Clubs of Miami is named Alex Rodriguez-Roig who said that when A-Rod was a boy, the club in his area (one of seven in Miami-Dade County) "gave him a lot of opportunity to develop, not only as an athlete, but as a person, and he acknowledges that and appreciates that and therefore gives back to the organization that helped him out when he was a child. He's grounded and giving."

Instead of becoming arrogant or complacent due to his enormous success, A-Rod, says Rodriguez-Roig, manages to avoid "flying, the think-you're-on-top-of-the-world kind of thing, but he takes that opportunity to help others.

"A lot of people [after achieving success] grow up and move on; he grew up but didn't move on—he remembers where he got his start. Not a lot of people of his caliber do that. He's the kind of guy that says, 'You know what, this is the place that I grew up and this is the place I want to make sure provides opportunities for other kids to grow up and have a successful life.'"

To this day, Rodriguez "comes around quite often" during the off-season to do special events such as taking part in a Christmas party at the club for the kids, with a generous Santa Rodriguez providing "tons of gifts."

In 2006, the club was building an education center to be named after Rodriguez, a $1.5 million project, which reflects his belief that there is more to life than just sports. Rodriguez-Roig said that A-Rod's attitude was "now [having already built a baseball field at the club] it's time to do the education stuff. He's always giving."[11]

TOO GOOD TO BE TRUE

Even earlier, he had shown flashes of thoughtfulness and grandiosity. When he was sent to play in the Instructional League not long after signing a very profitable contract, a sporting goods company gave him a great deal of baseball equipment. He promptly turned most of it over to teammates who he felt needed it more than he did.[12]

Clark Kellogg, basketball standout, called Rodriguez "a devout Christian . . . who drinks milk instead of beer, calls his mother five times a week, shows respect for his teammates, and signs—even encourages—autographs." For that matter, he was in the majors before he was of legal age to drink in some states. Kellogg went on to state that Rodriguez is willing to "embrace the responsibility" of being a role model, calling him the "rare athlete who understands—and cares—that his every move will be emulated by young fans." Further, he stated that Rodriguez's life is spent shooting for "a higher standard of excellence."[13] Rodriguez is the antithesis of sports stars who neither claim nor accept responsibility for being a role model.

His autobiography's focus was, understandably, children and the teaching of four vital areas of life and life skills: reading, math, physical fitness, and citizenship. Rodriguez comes off as a baseball Renaissance man, interested in a wide range of sports and subjects, including basketball, boating—he owned a boat named *Sweet Swing*—golf, a diverse range of music and art—he is said to have a fascination with Leonardo da Vinci and loves hip-hop music as well as Frank Sinatra tunes—and having taken college classes in creative writing and political science.[14]

Even when he became enormously wealthy, he wrote that money was not what his life was about, that money simply permitted him "to travel, to learn first hand from experts, and to meet interesting people. But at the end of the day it doesn't make me feel better inside." He added that "using money in a positive way" did make him feel better. After his 1996 donation to the Miami Boys Club to help rebuild their baseball field, he stated that, as a kid, he "couldn't afford a soda," and now "handing that check to Eddie [Rodriguez] . . . felt right and good." Since then, he has sponsored many other philanthropic ventures.[15]

MOM'S AND DAD'S INFLUENCES

He credited his mother with "a good foundation" of humility and said his mother has instilled in him the concept that money and even fame were meaningless if a person did not remain "the same person" he or she was before being inundated in a deluge of loot and glory.[16]

Therefore, it would be shocking to see him with countless thick-as-rattlesnakes gold necklaces draped around his neck, befitting a rap star or certain NBA players. He once said, "I don't like gold; it's not me." As Kellogg wrote, "He has maturity beyond his years and demonstrates rock-solid character attributes many call 'intangibles.'" Kellogg also quoted Lou Piniella as saying, "I haven't seen anybody as polished all the way around as he is."[17]

Rodriguez candidly admitted that he had been told that he was "far from a perfect child" and that he, being the baby of the family, had been spoiled by his father, Victor. When Alex did not get his way, he would "flop onto the floor and burst into a screaming, kicking, temper tantrum." Because his mother was working on a General Motors assembly line, leaving the house at 4:00 A.M., Victor was the default babysitter. At that time, the Rodriguezes owned a Manhattan shoe store and lived behind it. There, armed with an oversize red plastic bat, Alex would chase after any pitch within his reach, "often breaking things," and also toss a rubber ball against a "hallway wall for hours."[18]

Having developed his interest in baseball due to his father's influence, he once stated, "I always wanted to be like my dad, but my mom is my role model." He would continue to live with his mother during his off-seasons, sharing a bedroom with his German shepherd, a gift from Jose Canseco, which Alex named Ripper (as an homage to Cal Ripken Jr.), until 1996. Only then did he move from home, and even then he stayed in the Miami area, near his mother, the person he considered to be his inspiration in life.

When he did move away from home and bought his own residence, it was rather modest; containing four bedrooms, it was hardly palatial. The ranch house, part of a gated development in Kendall, is situated one street over from his mother's house in their South Miami neighborhood.

Lourdes encouraged Alex to play baseball and noted, "He was very interested from the time he was a child and just wasn't interested in anything else." Still, she insisted he grasp a key life lesson: "I don't care if you turn out to be a terrible ballplayer. I just want you to be a good person."[19]

Rodriguez became indefatigable when it came to signing endless autographs. He also has been known to toss in "a personal note to the signature." The fastidious Rodriguez also takes care to sign legibly, unlike some stars who peremptorily and "carelessly slap" their autographs down.[20] The way Rodriguez painstakingly signs is emblematic of the way he runs his life in general.

Meantime, his concerned mother hardly needed to fret about him turning out to be a poor player, but she had to be concerned about the pressure he would experience as early as his high school days. His coach at Westminster Christian, Rich Hofman, commented, "You can't imagine the pressure he had to go through. We had big crowds everywhere just to see him play." On top of that, recalled Hofman, the pitchers threw to him as if he represented the final out in the World Series. "I've never seen a player command so much attention, yet he's handled it with a great deal of humility." He even effortlessly handled the intense scrutiny of the "crush of agents and scouts everywhere we've gone."[21]

PRESSURE AND DRIVE

A-Rod has, for years now, been aware of the pressure on him to perform well (especially in the clutch), but he feels he has the drive and determination to meet those challenges.

Well aware of the figurative bounty on his head from childhood on, he also was appreciative that his mother helped alleviate the situation by informing him not to worry and to simply be himself.

Rodriguez already knew how to deal with the media, being articulate without coming off as glib. After the 1994 season, he had taken classes conducted by a media consultant that helped improve his verbal prowess and his dealings with the press. He determinedly was grooming himself in every facet of baseball life to become first class.

Former teammate Joey Cora said he believes that Rodriguez is almost obsessed to be the best player ever by the time he hangs up his spikes. Then, employing liberal hyperbole, Cora commented, "He'll do whatever it takes to get there, whatever is asked. If it means taking your mother out at second base, he'll do it."[22]

Tom Grieve agreed, "You look into the workouts that he has all winter long. Players don't come out and say, 'I push myself and I'm obsessive because I want to be the greatest player, and when I retire I want to hold all the records.' Those are things you don't [say], at least if you're Alex Rodriguez—some players might say those kind of things—because it just doesn't sound good, it sounds selfish. But unless you're driven and unless you have those personal goals, you don't become the best, or one of the best, players in baseball. I think that's what drives him—the competition and the intense desire, in my mind, to be the greatest player ever."[23]

His intense will to win was evident as early as the age of five when he played baseball on an informal team against kids from other neighborhoods. "I couldn't handle losing," he confessed. After a defeat, he would race home "crying angry tears." Then, in the darkness of his bedroom at night, he would devise ways of winning the next time out.[24]

Charles Zabransky, a longtime Yankees clubhouse attendant, said that often "when a guy's a good hitter and comes to the Yankees, he can't produce because the pressure's too great, and Rodriguez's under pressure and that's a problem."[25]

In the meantime, Rodriguez's high school coach, Rich Hofman, recounted a story that vividly typified young Alex's competitive ways. Alex failed in his first couple of trips to the plate against a tough pitcher for Brooksville Hernando High, prompting the pitcher to taunt Alex, who replied in kind. Later he came through, drawing a walk and legging out an infield hit on sheer determination. "He and this guy were really jaw-ing at each other, and we went to the top of the eighth and they were still going at each other a little bit. It was a game within a game. This guy threw him a fastball, and Alex deposited it deep over the left-field fence and we won in extra innings. I thought that was an extraordinary effort. He was not going to be denied; he willed himself into winning a game for us."[26]

Later in life, he learned to tolerate defeat better. When he came in second to Juan Gonzalez for the MVP Award in 1996, he was upset but not depressed. For one thing, he knew he had the respect of his peers. Philosophically, Rodriguez wrote in his autobiography that there was no sense in being bitter. He also persisted in his view that personal accom-plishments and stats are secondary to winning.

HURT PRIDE

Rodriguez frankly stated that he was quite disappointed at the MVP rebuke, evidence that his competitive nature was still afire. He revealed that, although he had tried not to think about the voting the night prior to the results hitting the public, in an attempt to convince himself that it was not all *that* important, he struggled to sleep well—he truly was psyched up for the MVP announcement. He made no attempt to hide just how much this honor meant to him; losing the MVP hurt deeply.

It truly would have been sweet, and a boon to his pride, to win the award. At this point, only two men of Dominican descent had ever won an MVP, George Bell in 1987 for the Toronto Blue Jays and Sammy Sosa in 1998 for the Chicago Cubs; Oakland's Miguel Tejada would go on to win the 2002 MVP. Make no mistake, Rodriguez *did* consider himself to be a Dominican deep down. He commented that although he was born in New York and grew up in Miami, with his parents coming from the Dominican Republic, his loyalty was with that nation.

Rodriguez exhibits and exudes his pride in how he handles himself, too. For instance, in his autobiography he recounted a time early in 1997 when he committed a ninth-inning throwing error against the Red Sox that cost the Mariners the last out of the inning and, ultimately in extra innings, the game. He wrote that he was proud of his resiliency as he doubled in his next at bat. He also noted how he "stood tall" after the game, facing up to and answering "every reporter's question, basically admitting I messed up and couldn't wait to get out there tomorrow. I gained a measure of respect that day."[27]

Later that year, he felt that he lost some of his dignity after throwing his bat in frustration. Eddie Rodriguez immediately called him on the clubhouse phone, notifying Alex to talk to him after the game. "I don't want to see you doing that stuff any more," he later scolded. Overall, Alex has his emotions under control. Eddie recalled once in Chicago when Alex slid headfirst into first base on a groundout and the ump blew the call. Alex's reaction, one of incredulity, got him thumbed. Another ejection came with the Jason Varitek incident. "I think those are the only two times. You don't see him complaining."[28]

When the Mariners dropped 85 games in 1998, he remained proud, pleased that he took each game and every at bat as if they were meaningful in the standings, as if Seattle was in contention. He said he attempted to give 100 percent at all times.

So many of the game's greats have been motivated by pride and the will to please themselves and/or a parent. It has been written that Ty Cobb was such a driven force because he was trying to prove to his father, already dead by a shotgun blast at the hands of his wife, that he was a success. Likewise, Rodriguez has stated he always had the desire to make his mother proud.

Rodriguez first met his hero, Cal Ripken Jr., when the Orioles star was in spring training camp in Florida and Alex was still in high school. Highly impressed that Ripken already had heard of him, Rodriguez soaked up advice. The two most vital lessons he learned were to work hard and to respect the game of baseball.[29] He also must have soaked up Ripken's constant desire to be on the field, not on the bench; Rodriguez played in every one of his team's contests in 1998, 2001, 2002, and 2005 and sat out only one game in 2003.

A-ROD'S AURA AND POPULARITY

Once a shy child, Rodriguez has molded himself into a man who is equally comfortable on a stool by his locker or on ESPN in the *Budweiser Hot Seat*. He is also equally at ease wearing New York Yankees pinstripes as he is in one of his many Armani suits, just as one could easily find his face on the cover of *Sports Illustrated* or *Gentleman's Quarterly*. He once stated that his basic sartorial rule is "you can never be overdressed." He believes that respect comes to the well-dressed man and once joked, "You can mess with my cars or my house. Just don't mess with my clothes." He felt a player was more than simply being, say, a power hitter, "You have to speak well, behave well, and dress well."[30] In short, sloppiness, in any form, on or off the playing field is anathema to Rodriguez.

Thus, his overall aura is, according to Steve Smith, who once managed Rodriguez in the minors, "like a president."[31] One writer said part of his popularity, beyond his movie star persona, stemmed from the fact that "he smiles like a kid on vacation." People are attracted to his magnetism; he receives 500 letters per week from fans, and even more kids clamor daily for his signature. Not only that, but he thanks autograph seekers for wanting him to sign. "He appears to be as perfect as a hot fudge sundae."[32]

His family members paid tribute to the kind of man Alex became. Lourdes commented, "Setbacks and tribulations never stopped Alex from pursuing his dream" and that at no time were his goals out of focus. His sister, Susy, lauded his hard work for everything he attained, remembering how even when he was a youngster in front of the TV he would be lifting weights. Next, his older brother, Joe, recalled spending time with Alex, who wanted nothing more than to have Joe "throw him [Wiffle] balls that he'd hit with a plastic bat." From the very start, he said, Alex "had that drive."[33]

David Segui was impressed with A-Rod's ability to go all out, all the time. "Fans think that because of the money we make, we should be at our best every game. But we're still human beings. Our minds and bodies don't always perform at our best. Except for Alex. He forces himself to be at the top level every single game."[34]

James Colzie, who spent time with the Montreal Expos organization, once opined, "What you see is what you get with Alex. Money hasn't changed him. There's no dark side to him."[35]

THE INFLUENCE OF FAME

That begs the question: Has fame changed him? Rich Hofman declared, "It *has* to. I mean, I don't think it changed so much his very core of who he is, but how you live and what you do obviously changes. You need more privacy, you need security, you can't be an average guy any more walking on the street. But I always look at him as just Alex. A lot of people worship him, but I just enjoy the relationship. I'm not in awe of him as a person; he's still my player. Now as he's matured and gotten older, we're more like peers—it's more of an equal relationship in a lot of ways and that's fun. I think he still looks at me as his coach."[36]

Tom Grieve said, "I don't know that you can have the kind of fame that he had and not change in some way. I don't know that a human being is capable of that. Is he the kid that he was when he was a rookie? No, he's more confident now, more outgoing, he takes more of a leadership role. Back then, Lou Piniella was a very dominating personality as a manger and there was Ken Griffey and Jay Buhner on Seattle, so all he had to do was blend in. Now, when you look at his off-the-field activities and the business investments that he has, I don't think there's any reason to think that he hasn't changed, *but* I don't know that his basic personality—who he is and the friends that he keeps—has changed." He feels A-Rod's old friends probably would say he "hasn't changed that much, and I think that's one of his strong suits, the fact that he remains close and loyal to the people who were close to him when he was growing up."[37]

Bill Henderson, coach and athletic director at Westminster Christian, said that in many ways "there are similarities with him today and the Alex that was back then. Obviously, fame and some money change you in some ways, [they] force change, but Alex came from a modest, to say the least, upbringing. I just remember a kid who was barely able to attend Westminster and rarely remember seeing family members able to attend any games because of working two or three jobs."

Henderson, a Detroit Tigers first-round draft pick out of Westminster in 1987 and a four-year veteran of pro ball, said, "The story that sort of sums it up in terms of how his financial life has changed is [from] one particular day when I mentioned [to Alex], 'I have some old stuff [equipment] hanging around. You're welcome to have anything you want.'" Alex, then in 10th grade, asked for Henderson's metal spikes. "Not only did he come over and get them, but he had to go way out of his way and hitch a ride to come pick up these $80 spikes that were going on three years old. It's ironic now. Needless to say, nowadays I think he could probably buy himself some spikes." Actually, he added, "Nike would send him 5,000 spikes if he told them to." Back then, however, getting the shoes was a sort of vicarious big-league experience.[38]

MOTIVATION

Rodriguez's introspective view revealed that he motivates himself by constantly reminding himself "that fame is fleeting" and that he always acts and thinks as if he had just "played my last baseball game." He insists he will avoid the twin pitfalls of arrogance and complacency and that his aim is to remain a great citizen. He even indicated that if injury terminated his career prematurely, his main concern was for people to like him for the person he is, for his inner qualities.

When A-Rod won the 2005 MVP over Boston's David Ortiz, who had come off a stunning World Series victory in 2004, Rodriguez commented,

"I would certainly trade his World Series championship for this MVP trophy. That's the only reason I play baseball. It's what I'm consumed to do right now."[39]

Likewise, Rodriguez is such a perfectionist, winning his second MVP, to become one of just four men to win the award with two different clubs, did not make him less determined. Nor did he feel winning such an honor would end criticism that he does not perform in the clutch or that he is not a winner.

"We can win three World Series; with me, it's never going to be over. I think my benchmark is so high that no matter what I do, it's never going to be enough, and I understand that. Maybe when I retire is when all critics and all that kind of stuff will end."[40]

Even though most people perceive Rodriguez as a superstar, in his own mind there lingers a nagging issue of how critics see him. The fear that he might end his career as another Ernie Banks who never played in a World Series is palpable. Allegations also have been made from time to time that Rodriguez is a selfish player. Likewise, he has been accused of putting up great regular-season numbers but less than glittering statistics in the clutch.

DEDICATION TO HIS CRAFT

Should A-Rod never win a World Series, it would be folly to blame it on any lack of assiduousness on Rodriguez's part. According to writer Joe Christensen, Rodriguez usually showed up for 7:00 night-game starts by 1:30 for extra batting practice and to study his swing on videotape.[41] After ball games, he analyzes everything at home, where he is said to have a veritable library of videos, focusing mainly on opposing pitchers and tendencies of enemy hitters to aid him on defense.

Highly respected Texas Rangers hitting coach Rudy Jaramillo commended Rodriguez for his splendid work ethic, which was as regimented as it was regular. When A-Rod was still with Texas, Jaramillo outlined Rodriguez's daily grind to painstakingly prepare himself for each contest, displaying boundless vitality. "At 6:15 I have my little program with Alex Rodriguez that we go through, getting him ready. He does tee work, he hits breaking balls, he hits live hitting, and he wants situations, and he gets himself ready for the game until about five till seven in our cage." When done with the A-Rod show, it nearly would be time for the opening pitch, and finally he felt fully prepared for the ensuing game. He quietly would go about such preparation day after day after day.[42]

Tom Grieve said, "The one anecdote that might give you a little bit of an idea about the kind of player he is—the first year he was here [in Texas], we were in last place and the last three games of the year were in Anaheim. On the last day of the season there was no batting practice—basically it was, 'Show up, play the game, and let's go home.' Bucky Dent was our infield coach, and probably 45 minutes before the game—the Angels weren't going to take batting practice—Alex comes out on the field with Mark Teixeira, Michael Young, and Hank Blalock, all young players early in their careers, and they went through infield practice—when it meant nothing. It was Alex's idea; his thought was these kids are going to be a big part of our future here and let's start right now getting ready for next year with the way we're going to do things. And that was a pretty impressive thing to watch."[43]

Such dedication belies the widely held concept that everything has come easy, with nearly ho-hum effortlessness for the handsome and seemingly tireless Rodriguez. Although he always has had natural talent—one imagines he was the kid who was selected first in *any* pickup game he ever took part in—he has worked hard at his trade.

By his own evaluation, some of the elements of his success are his pride in his job and his focus. He was especially proud of his toil and energy down seasons' stretch drives. Obviously, that was not an easy task when his Texas team often was buried in last place, but Rodriguez pushed on relentlessly. Like a strange mix between a thoroughbred and a workhorse, he majestically toiled in 162, 162, and 161 contests over his three seasons under the energy-sapping, boiling, midday Texas sun.

He once commented that he possessed an unbelievable amount of motivation to improve and to do so on a daily basis. "Integrity-wise, I cannot allow whether the team is winning or not to affect me. I'm going to give maximum effort. I have to look at myself every day and judge myself on my work ethic."[44]

Rodriguez is so dedicated, he puts himself through a daily regimen that would put most players to shame. When many hitters are lounging around in the clubhouse with about an hour or so before game time, Rodriguez is taking an extra session of hitting with his hitting coach. He took extra practice against breaking balls and extra hitting off the tee as well.

Like so many superstars from Ty Cobb to Pete Rose, when it comes to winning, Rodriguez has sought any edge he can find. He once stated that he would do anything in order to win. "I'll even cheat to win," he once said.[45]

Although Brady Anderson is widely believed to be the first player to wear the Rollerblade elbow pad, Rodriguez shortly followed suit. As Anderson once observed, when a player gets hit on the elbow, at the very least his swing will be impaired for some time, and, of course, in the very worst scenario, the player will miss time sitting on the bench or even on the disabled list. Rodriguez, then, feels like Anderson, who commented that he would stand as close to the plate as he wanted, refusing to give in to pitchers or fear the repercussions of being struck by a pitch.

As far back as his high school days, Rodriguez worked hard at devising ways to win and to improve. Knowing professional ballplayers were banned from using aluminum bats, he gave them up in high school, even though those bats provided him with additional raw power. He insisted on using wood bats to acclimate himself to the conditions pros face.[46]

MONETARY MATTERS

Dr. Charles Maher is the sport psychologist and director of Psychological Services for the Cleveland Indians and Cavaliers and has served in similar positions for the White Sox and Yankees over a 15-year period. His credentials are sterling, as he also has worked as a sport psychologist with players from the New York Jets, New England Patriots, and the Cleveland Browns. In addition, he is a tenured full professor at Rutgers University.

A player such as the intense, driven Albert Belle once insisted a clause be placed in his contract guaranteeing that he be the highest-paid player in the game. He also demanded that his contract include a clause guaranteeing that if, after a period of time, another player signed elsewhere in baseball for more money, his contract would be adjusted upward to ensure he stays among, say, the top three salaries in baseball.

Such a stance can influence players' performances, as a happy player tends to be a productive player and vice versa (or so, at least, a player might argue). Dr. Maher explained that with some players it is not the money as much as the need to boost self-esteem. He elaborated that some ballplayers become distracted if they discover they are not among, for example, the top five money earners in the game, and such a distraction hurts their performance.

So, even if a player was hitting .333 with a passel of homers and RBIs and was hauling home a fortune every payday, he *still* might suffer from pay envy if he felt he was underappreciated. This may well stem from the fact that such a man is unable to nudge ego issues aside; these men become miserable, and it shows.

It does not, however, have to be that way. Dr. Maher sited Alex Rodriguez as an exception. "He has a top salary, but he has a passion for the game. He plays it, and he has good self-esteem. I think if he went down from the top salary to the fifth highest or the tenth highest, I don't think it would effect him."[47]

Texas Rangers owner Tom Hicks so coveted Rodriguez, he offered him the highest salary in the history of sports in 2001, signing him on December 11 to a staggering $252 million, 10-year contract. Hicks felt that he simply *had* to get him under contract, regardless of the price, believing Rodriguez would turn Texas into a perennial contender.

Rodriguez's reaction to the deal was revelatory. "This is the first time I've been singled out like this. It's as though I'm walking around with a sign on my neck that says '252' [million dollars]." He asked rhetorically, "How will I react?" then answered his own question, saying that having never before been in such a situation, he honestly did not know, but he thought he would adapt and handle it well.[48]

During the December 12, 2000, press conference announcing the contract, Rodriguez also pointed out that he felt blessed. There was no false modesty involved; he knew he had worked diligently to get where he was, but he also was well aware that many people in all walks of life work hard. He said he believed there should be only one person who merited such money, the one who could come up with a cure for cancer.

On February 21, 2001, he commented that he had "always been the underdog who's gone out and played well and tried to show everybody that I'm worth being the number one pick or a 40–40 guy. Now, there's this 252 tag over my head." On the other hand, he added that he actually relished "the responsibility that goes along with it, both on and off the field."[49]

Entering the season, Rodriguez remembered how Griffey Jr. once had warned him of the expectations and woes that accompany the signing of huge contracts. He therefore worked out with renewed zeal to combat any possible letdown.

Inking the leviathan contract did not, in fact, seem to effect him; certainly no complacency set in. Inevitably writers whipped out their calculators, however, coming up with such outlandish figures as A-Rod will earn roughly $136,000 per game or $15,111 per inning.

What they did not factor in were the countless grueling years of preparation and diligence he had spent (and would continue to spend) developing his craft, the many months away from home, such as those spent during the all-important, yet sometimes tedious, spring training camps, nor the myriad minutes he spent studying the game.

The bottom line was, of course, $20+ million per year with the Rangers was a lot of moolah, and the contract was destined to attract those anxious to rip Rodriguez. His Texas manager, Buck Showalter, summed it up, "He can't win. You may win a battle, but you're going to lose the war. I think he understands it and what people say and perceive [about him]. Does it hurt? Yeah."[50]

Eddie Rodriguez agrees with Showalter that many who rip Alex are "on a jealousy trip and are unfair. For example, he hits a two-run homer and the next time he hits a ground ball and they boo him, blaming everything on him. He's going to have to learn to live with it. What people don't realize is that he's a human being like everybody else; he can get hurt. I always tell him, 'You're 6' 3", 240 pounds, and you make $40 million; there's a lot of people who don't even have time to live, look at those kids who die of cancer—you've got to be grateful. All that booing, just sweat it out and swing the bat and that's it. Then they're going to start cheering.'" Furthermore, the jealousy and criticism have made Alex more guarded and more protective of himself. "You've got to. People who only see him from far away make judgments," said Eddie, who believes Alex, in turn, might find it difficult to trust those he does not know well. "Especially in New York, especially the media in New York." New Yorkers, he explained, "want a championship, and they are paying to win the championship" but have come up empty of late.[51]

Other defenders of Rodriguez pointed out that in return for the money, A-Rod supplied Texas with a lot of punch—52, 57, and 47 homers over the three seasons he spent with the Rangers, leading the league each year, a feat done only twice since the Babe Ruth era. Further, he led the league as a Ranger in slugging percentage, homers, and runs scored in the same season, joining only four other men who managed this over the last 50 years. Clearly, money was not the driving force in his life; his pride and performance were.

Many outsiders were impressed with how he could shove aside money matters once the contract was signed, but those who knew Rodriguez understood how focused he is. Bill Henderson opined that when he is alone with Rodriguez he seems just like the same guy he knew as a kid. Hofman did not find Alex to be a typical player because he is among the elite, the kind of player who is bombarded by so many demands from marketing to media matters and more. Regardless, Hofman believes A-Rod is incredibly focused and adept at managing his life.

"Most human beings, whether it's golf or a diet or whatever, tend to indulge. He has some self-discipline that you and I probably don't have, where a certain time of year hits and he's going to work out twice a day, he's going to hit balls, field balls. That discipline and focus is something that is very, very rare."[52]

Rodriguez often has said that he is able to ignore outside disturbances, even large ones such as an impending players' strike at the end of August 2002. He had become accustomed to distractions and could cast them off once he heard the umpire bark, "Play ball!"

One negative side effect of his contract occurred when he did a radio interview and commented that he did not think his old buddy Derek Jeter would command as much money when he next signed a Yankees contract because he lacked the power A-Rod had and was beneath Rodriguez defensively as well. Not too long after those inflammatory words, he turned up the heat and once more took a "snipe at Jeter." In an interview Rodriguez did with a writer for *Esquire* magazine, he was quoted as saying that Jeter was fortunate to have so many other talented players surrounding him and claimed Jeter never had to take charge and lead the team. "He can just go and play and have fun. He hits second—that's totally different than third or fourth in the lineup. You go into New York, you wanna stop Bernie [Williams] and [Paul] O'Neill. You never say, 'Don't let Derek beat you.' He's never your concern."[53]

Apology or not, the two never again would be as close. Whatever possessed Rodriguez to take such a harsh, out-of-left-field verbal poke at Jeter is not totally clear; some speculated it was simply an inevitable outburst of the ego so many stars exude, whereas others said it was a display of a figurative sibling rivalry or of World Series ring envy. What is certain is Jeter resented the comments and spoke privately with Rodriguez. True, Rodriguez, the all-around better player of the two, should have had nothing to prove, but many have speculated that Rodriguez might be a bit jealous of Jeter, winner of the 1996 Rookie of the Year Award (A-Rod, due to the number of games he had played in 1994 and 1995, was not eligible for that trophy in 1996), and envious, too, of Jeter's four World Series rings.

Make no mistake, sports figures do have strong egos, albeit in varying degrees. Larry Bowa, who led the National League in fielding six times at shortstop, said, "Usually your best [young] athletes gravitate to that position [shortstop]. So obviously all those Latin players who play shortstop were the best athletes on their youth teams. That's why guys like [Miguel] Tejada, [Omar] Vizquel, A-Rod, everyone wants to play there. It's almost a status thing." Rodriguez himself admitted that he takes the most pride in his glove work. "The first thing I have to think about," he commented, "is my defense. It may not get the highlights on ESPN or *Baseball Tonight*, but it may be where I can help this ball club the most." Therefore, Bowa certainly appears correct about two issues: Many players from Latin

America love the game and focus on the glamour spot in the middle of the diamond and the spotlight, and those who evolve and become skilled, confident players develop a figurative swagger.[54]

INTENSITY AND MORE SCRUTINY

Rodriguez is much more serious than playful. Bill Henderson, who saw Rodriguez up close at Westminster Christian, feels Alex does have a playful side, "but it always seemed like it was all business between the lines and in terms of working, getting extra batting practice or ground balls after practice. If it was a water break, he'd definitely cut up and joke around, but once it was between the lines, he was all business."[55]

Celebrity worshippers in the United States are notoriously fickle, delighting in building up their idols, vicariously relishing in their accomplishments, then, perversely, searching for, or at times even manufacturing, a chink in their heroes' otherwise glistening armor.

Rodriguez has, by and large, remained *somewhat* immune from such fault finding, maintaining a clean image, but certainly more so early on in his career (B.C., before the contract), to be sure. By 2006, though, he saw himself as being despised, stating that "everyone hates me."[56]

Mark Teixeira felt that if A-Rod felt under more scrutiny and even was lambasted due to his fame, he was still somehow able to execute his job on the diamond while handling all the pressure that is attendant to such fame. "I think there's a lot of jealousy that goes on in the game. He's the highest paid player in the game, he's probably the most talented player in the game, so any time you have that combination you're going to have a lot of players and a lot of people that are jealous of him."[57]

Alex Rodriguez-Roig, executive director of the Boys and Girls Clubs of Miami, stated, "Sometimes when a person like [Alex] with the big controversy [concerning] the big contract and the envy starts kicking in and people start making things up. But the bottom line is: Yes, of course, he makes a ton of money. There's nothing illegal about that; that's actually great."[58] Especially, he said, when he takes some of that money and gives to charities in an age when so many athletes do not help their communities. Some athletes, he pointed out, will donate, but they do so merely by cutting a check, but Rodriguez is a rare hands-on kind of player who gives both money and time, spending both lavishly on Miami youth, and that, Rodriguez-Roig feels, says a lot about the superstar.

In 2006, Showalter said there has been criticism directed at Rodriguez for quite some time. He says many people are envious of Rodriguez despite his devotion to the game he so dearly loves. Therefore, constantly in the limelight, he strives "to live up to the covenant of being a big-league player, and a *great* big-league player. People like to shoot at things they can't do themselves. Thank goodness there's somebody there as talented as he is and cares about the way he carries himself." However, well aware of some people's envy, Rodriguez seldom drops his guard and stays within his small circle of trusted friends.

Although Rodriguez, like any other superstar, cannot entirely trust new people he meets, he remains loyal to those who go way back with him. As Showalter put it, "He's got a circle of people that have grown up with him, that know him and know that his heart's pure. We're all like that to some extent, we just aren't on the front page. I'm happy for him that he's got people around him that he knows [and who] trust him."[59]

Rodriguez tries to shun inflammatory situations for the most part. Consider, for example, how he deftly handled a volatile situation when he joined the New York Yankees. An established All-Star at shortstop with credentials that would justify prima-donna demands on how he was treated, Rodriguez was smooth when asked how he and fellow superstar shortstop Derek Jeter could coexist. They *would* get along, he said.

A-Rod's image took a hit though during a Yankees versus Red Sox game on July 24, 2004, when the already combustible relationship between the teams got even more explosive when a memorable brawl broke out.

After getting plunked by a pitch, the normally unflappable Rodriguez squawked at the Red Sox pitcher, Bronson Arroyo, causing catcher Jason Varitek to, in turn, jaw with and eventually physically confront Rodriguez, leading to a veritable 12-round bout that sprawled across the Fenway field.

Later, Rodriguez commented that he had "no regrets about doing what I did. Obviously, it's not good for our game, so I'm remorseful about that . . . but in the heat of the moment, sometimes you've got to throw down."[60] The following spring, Boston's Trot Nixon, clearly not a Rodriguez admirer, labeled him a "clown."

Tom Grieve believes A-Rod "is a lightning rod because he's got a target on his back because of his contract. . . . With that contract comes expectations that can never be met. He can't hit 100 home runs and knock in 200 runs and hit .425—he just can't do that."[61]

Some people theorized that it was almost as if A-Rod had become so uncharacteristically combative as if to dispel the notion that he was too good, too soft, and too much of a "pretty boy" to dirty himself in a scuffle. Normally, during so-called basebrawls, Rodriguez, like many of the game's levelheaded pacifists, tends to break up fights or remain on the periphery of any skirmish, far from the epicenter. That was not so in the

Varitek incident, resulting in many of his critics seemingly taking delight in witnessing Rodriguez's imperial facade slipping, even if for only a few fleeting minutes.

Eddie Rodriguez said that Alex is sometimes "too passive. I love when he had the fight with Jason Varitek; I want to see the other side. Like the other day when he hit a grand slam [in 2006] and he flipped the bat [flamboyantly and joyfully]—Manny [Ramirez] and 90 percent of the ballplayers do [gestures] 15 times worse and they don't even notice, but just because it was Alex, [catcher Paul Lo Duca] noticed it." Alex, said Eddie, "was just exuberant because his slam jolted him out of his recent doldrums. Lo Duca said something to him and he responded right back to him. I love to see that side of him because people push him too much, sometimes push him to the limit."[62]

Grieve also feels there are a few things A-Rod has said or done that he regrets, such as the time he knocked "the ball out of Bronson Arroyo's hand. That just looked terrible. Knowing Alex a little bit and the pride that he has in the way he plays the game, that had to be something that really killed him, to see himself embarrassed in all the replays, by all the commentators, and by all the Red Sox players. At the time, he felt like he was making a move that would help his team win."[63]

Grieve, of course, was referring to the controversy concerning the ill-fated move he made in the 2004 American League Championship Series, once more versus the hated Red Sox. In Game 6, Boston's Curt Schilling lasted through seven innings, departing with a 4–1 lead. Then, in the eighth, a play took place that no doubt will haunt Rodriguez throughout his entire career. After Jeter had singled in a run to cut the lead to two, A-Rod entered the batter's box to face Bronson Arroyo. He tapped a harmless grounder back toward the mound. Arroyo fielded it and dashed toward the base path to retire Rodriguez. As Arroyo was applying the tag to Rodriguez with the ball in his glove, A-Rod tomahawked at his glove, much like an illegal move in hockey known as slashing, causing the ball to become dislodged and to roll down the right-field line, allowing Jeter to score all the way from first base and Rodriguez to advance to second, where he represented the potential game-tying run.

Seconds later, however, the umpires met and, although the first base umpire, Randy Marsh, had been screened on the play and did not have a clear view, the other umps got the call right. Rodriguez had interfered with Arroyo and was automatically out, and Jeter was ordered to trot back to first base, costing the Yankees a run and prompting a torrent of beer bottles onto the field.

Rodriguez's actions were labeled "bush" and "a cheap stunt." Dan Shaughnessy wrote that "A-Rod hurt his reputation further by standing on second, raising his arms, and folding his hands on top of his helmet as if to say, 'What did I do?'" Clearly, his denials and protestations of innocence were rather lame. The following day, Schilling said scornfully, "That was junior high school baseball right there, at best."[64] Then in October 2005, perhaps the most serious threat to taint his reputation came along.

The same month that Rodriguez won his second MVP, he also went on record for the first time about a *New York Daily News* story that revealed he had been at an underground New York poker club along with Phil Hellmuth, a professional card player. In a sidebar on *ESPN.com*, a contrite Rodriguez was quoted as saying, "Obviously, it wasn't the right thing to do. In retrospect, it's probably a place I shouldn't have gone."[65] Another account also revealed that "Alex Rodriguez was cautioned by the New York Yankees that playing poker in illegal clubs could be dangerous and harmful to his image, according to a newspaper report. On Oct. 2, the Daily News reported the star slugger had attended games at an underground club with Hellmuth."[66] Later, though, Rodriguez spoke with the media, stating, according to the ESPN Web site, "that the team had never really talked to him about it; his agent, Scott Boras, and the Yankees also denied that such a conversation took place." A-Rod also called going to the club "a dumb thing" and added he would not "be back to those places. I'm moving forward."[67]

It seems safe to say, for the most part, that Rodriguez, like Willy Loman, strongly feels the importance of being well liked, but new inflammatory issues raged in 2006, and A-Rod again found it difficult to be accepted. When he struggled in August, a *Sports Illustrated* writer worked on a story that painted a bleak portrait of Rodriguez's relationship with his Yankee teammates. The piece hit the newsstands with a theatrical thud right around the time the Yanks clinched their division and accused A-Rod of being "hard to motivate and harder to understand."

Writer Tom Verducci labeled Rodriguez as being a "baseball Narcissus" who would gaze at "his beautiful statistics" and called both his appearance and his game "wrinkle-free." However, Jason Giambi felt Joe Torre had coddled A-Rod and felt a confrontation to address Rodriguez's slump was in order. Giambi told Rodriguez he had to start coming through with clutch hits and claimed he does not even "know who he is," but that the upcoming playoffs would clear that up. Verducci also stated that Rodriguez refused to acknowledge his slump and was therefore "letting himself and the team down."[68]

On the very first day of Rodriguez's 2007 spring training he stirred the contents of a bubbling cauldron once more when he told the media that his relationship with Derek Jeter had cooled. Over the last three years he had denied such charges, insisting the two were still close friends. This time, however, he commented, "People start assuming that things are a lot worse than what they are, which they're not. But they're obviously not as great as they used to be. We were like blood brothers." When he was initially asked about his Jeter during the interview Rodriguez stated, "Let's make a contract: You don't ask me about Derek anymore and I promise I'll stop lying to all you guys."[69]

All things considered, the picture of the man is in reality a complex, abstract painting. Somehow, despite his generosity and boundless ability, he remained, to many, difficult to understand and disliked.

NOTES

1. Glenn Stout, *On the Field With . . . Alex Rodriguez* (New York: Little, Brown, 2002), 4.

2. Author's interview with Rich Hofman, May 3, 2006.

3. Author's interview with Eddie Rodriguez, July 6, 2006.

4. E-mail correspondence with Dr. Claudia Springer, May 2006.

5. Author's interview with Rich Hofman, May 3, 2006.

6. Author's interview with Tom Grieve, March 8, 2006.

7. Author's interview with Eddie Rodriguez, July 6, 2006.

8. Author's interview with Bill Henderson, July 2006.

9. Author's interview with Rich Hofman, May 3, 2006.

10. Alex Rodriguez and Greg Brown, *Hit a Grand Slam* (Dallas: Taylor, 1998), 2.

11. Author's interview with Alex Rodriguez-Roig, July 5, 2006.

12. Stout, *On the Field With . . . Alex Rodriguez*, 60.

13. Steve Riach, *Heart of a Champion: Profiles in Character*, with John Humphrey (Nashville, TN: Broadman and Holman, 2001), 13.

14. Michael Bradley, *Alex Rodriguez* (Tarrytown, NY: Benchmark Books, 2005), 10.

15. Rodriguez and Brown, *Hit a Grand Slam*, 38.

16. Mike Shalin, *Alex Rodriguez: A+ Shortstop* (Champaign, IL: Sports Publishing, 1999), 76.

17. Riach, *Heart of a Champion*, 13–15.

18. Rodriguez and Brown, *Hit a Grand Slam*, 6–7.

19. Stew Thornley, *Alex Rodriguez: Slugging Shortstop* (Minneapolis, MN: Lerner, 1998), 15.

20. Glen Macnow, *Sports Great, Alex Rodriguez* (Berkeley Heights, NJ: Enslow, 2002), 12.

21. Thornley, *Alex Rodriguez: Slugging Shortstop*, 24–25.

22. Tom Gage, "A-Rod Does It Better," *Baseball Digest*, October 2005, 23.

23. Author's interview with Tom Grieve, March 8, 2006.

24. Rodriguez and Brown, *Hit a Grand Slam*, 10.

25. Author's interview with Charles Zabransky, October 31, 2006.

26. Author's interview with Rich Hofman, May 3, 2006.

27. Rodriguez and Brown, *Hit a Grand Slam*.

28. Author's interview with Eddie Rodriguez, July 6, 2006.

29. Rodriguez and Brown, *Hit a Grand Slam*, 36.

30. Macnow, *Sports Great, Alex Rodriguez*, 46.

31. Riach, *Heart of a Champion*, 13.

32. Macnow, *Sports Great, Alex Rodriguez*, 44.

33. Rodriguez and Brown, *Hit a Grand Slam*, 38.

34. Macnow, *Sports Great, Alex Rodriguez*, 51.

35. Rodriguez and Brown, *Hit a Grand Slam*, 39.

36. Author's interview with Rich Hofman, May 3, 2006.

37. Author's interview with Tom Grieve, March 8, 2006.

38. Author's interview with Bill Henderson, July 2006.

39. Chris Snow, "Award lands in A-Rod's glove," *Boston Globe* (November 15, 2005), available at http://www.boston.com/sports/baseball/redsox/articles/2005/11/15/award_lands_in_a_rods_glove/.

40. Ibid.

41. Joe Christensen, *Alex Rodriguez* (Edina, MN: ABDO, 2004), 8.

42. Wayne Stewart, *Hitting Secrets of the Pros: Big-League Sluggers Reveal the Tricks of Their Trade* (New York: McGraw-Hill, 2004), 151.

43. Author's interview with Tom Grieve, March 8, 2006.

44. Bradley, *Alex Rodriguez*, 11.

45. Shalin, *Alex Rodriguez: A+ Shortstop*, 73.

46. Rodriguez and Brown, *Hit a Grand Slam*, 26.

47. Author's interview with Dr. Charles Maher, June 2002.

48. Rodriguez and Brown, *Hit a Grand Slam*, 38.

49. Kim Covert, *Alex Rodriguez* (Mankato, MN: Capstone Press, 2002), 40.

50. Author's interview with Buck Showalter, April 28, 2006.

51. Author's interview with Eddie Rodriguez, July 6, 2006.

52. Author's interview with Bill Henderson, July 2006.

53. Buster Olney, *The Last Night of the Yankee Dynasty* (New York: HarperCollins, 2004), 215.

54. Tim Wendel, *The New Face of Baseball: The 100-Year Rise and Triumph of Latinos in America's Favorite Sport* (New York: HarperCollins, 2003), 80–81.

55. Author's interview with Bill Henderson, July 2006.

56. Bob Nightengale, "New Look, Same Personality," *USA Today Sports Weekly*, April 26–May 2, 2006, 11.

57. Author's interview with Mark Teixeira, April 28, 2006.

58. Author's interview with Alexander Rodriguez-Roig, July 5, 2006.

59. Author's interview with Buck Showalter, April 28, 2006.

60. Dan Shaughnessy, *Reversing the Curse: Inside the 2004 Boston Red Sox* (New York: Houghton Mifflin, 2005), 144.

61. Author's interview with Tom Grieve, March 8, 2006.

62. Author's interview with Eddie Rodriguez, July 6, 2006.

63. Author's interview with Tom Grieve, March 8, 2006.

64. Shaughnessy, *Reversing the Curse*, 205–6.

65. "A-Rod's new deal: No more clubs," *ESPN.com* (November 14, 2005—sidebar), available at http://sports.espn.go.com/mlb/news/story?id=2223736.

66. "Report: A-Rod warned about playing poker," *NBCSports.com* (November 2, 2005), available at http://www.msnbc.msn.com/id/9896335/.

67. "A-Rod's new deal…"

68. Tom Verducci, "A-Rod Agonistes," *Sports Illustrated*, September 25, 2006, 37–44.

69. Art Martone, "A-Rod: Friendship with Jeter has 'cooled'," *Providence Journal: Projo Sports Blog* (February 19, 2007), available at http://www.beloblog.com/ProJo_Blogs/sportsblog/2007/02/arod_friendship_with_jeter_has.html.

Chapter 3

BECOMING A PRO, 1993–1995

Shortly after becoming a Mariner, Rodriguez flew to Seattle and met with established star Ken Griffey Jr., himself only 23. Typical of their age, they played video games, relaxed, and related to each other as fellow number one draft selections—Griffey Jr. in 1987—empathizing over the chaos and hype they had endured. There soon would be much more chaos and hype to follow.

There was still more baseball at the tail end of 1993 for Rodriguez as the Mariners shipped him off to Peoria, Arizona, to take part in the Instructional League. There, under the guidance of veteran big-league manager John McNamara, Rodriguez learned baseball the Mariners way while team officials monitored his progress. After seeing Rodriguez play in his first game, in which he robbed five batters of hits, McNamara marveled, "You couldn't ask for a better-played game of shortstop. The kid looks and plays mature." His hitting coach, Tommy Cruz, liked Rodriguez's offensive ability but said he would have to "get used to the hard stuff [fastballs] again." Having been force-fed so much junk and breaking balls by high schoolers, Rodriguez would have to retool his cut.[1] That would prove to be no problem at all.

The first mention of Rodriguez in the Mariners media guide came in 1994, and the reviews were a bit mixed. The three-paragraph item (by 2005, the data in the Yankees information and record guide consumed a whopping eight pages) stated he hit a microscopic .197 in the Arizona Instructional League, a league that invites top young big-league prospects out West during the late fall to showcase and work with them over a short schedule. He did, however, lead his "club in stolen bases (6) and committed just one error." It had been, as a matter of fact, his first brush with pro baseball.[2]

His first spring camp allowed him to see firsthand just how assiduously big leaguers work. Rodriguez would show up 30 minutes early for the squad's 10:00 A.M. practices. Only when he got there one day at 7:00 A.M. did he realize that for some dedicated players, such as Jay Buhner, arriving as much as three hours before the required time was not exactly considered early. For instance, two-time batting crown winner Edgar Martinez would remain after some practice sessions to work out on his own, sometimes staying as late as 6:00 P.M., four hours beyond the norm.[3]

Of course, it was not exactly as if Rodriguez was not a hard worker. After his stint in the Instructional League had ended the year prior, he returned to Miami, where he worked out throughout the winter "five hours a day running, lifting weights, and fielding grounders."[4] Then it was time to report to the Mariners.

From the big-league spring training camp, Rodriguez was shipped off to begin the season at the Class A Appleton, Wisconsin, farm club, skipping over the Rookie League. In Appleton, his independence and self-sufficiency came into play as he was, for the first meaningful period, on his own. He shared an apartment with a teammate and avoided distractions off the field at all costs.

Playing with the Foxes under manager Carlos Lezcano was to be the first of four whistle-stops he would make in his kaleidoscopic first full year as a professional ballplayer. Lezcano said having Alex "was a pleasure. I'm very happy for Alex's success; he's a true professional.

"He was very mature for his age. He handled himself very well and he was a very, very talented kid. At the level he way playing, he dominated. I think he could have competed in the big leagues right out of high school—with his ability he would have handled it. He's one of the few guys who could have done it." Still, Lezcano added that seasoning Rodriguez in the minors was the right call, "the best thing for him. You cannot rush a kid like that."

Alex, already displaying power, was playing with men as much as four years older. "He looked like he was [one of them] instead of a young guy. His body and his ability were way past his years." Lezcano said his biggest assets were "his God-given ability with the body that he was given, and his coordination at that age with that body was amazing, but, to me, his best tool was his brain. He knew how to handle himself and he was a quick learner. He had the ability, but he had the smarts to be able to develop quickly and do the right things.

"It's very hard to find those kinds of tools. [Some prospects] have tools but they don't have the maturity. Alex would get the information, store it, and then you could see him [utilize it] right in the game. It would take him one, two days, and he had it. That's very, very unusual in baseball players—they've got to make a few mistakes, it takes them a little longer, but [he] made [quick] adjustments. He was also focused all the time."

"You taught him something and he took it into the game right away; the fastest learner I ever had as a coach."[5]

Lezcano also was impressed with how respectful Rodriguez was of his mother when she visited to see him play. Lezcano teasingly would use his mother as leverage to make sure Alex, for example, showed up on time, "but he never did anything wrong. I'd say jokingly, like you tell a little kid, 'I'm going to tell your mother.'

His milestone first pro hit came on April 8, when he went two for four in his pro debut at Quad City. It did not take him too much longer to notch his first official homer as a pro, doing so with a 440-foot poke on April 24 versus Fort Wayne, Indiana.[6]

Rodriguez knew instantly that the ball he had just struck was headed out of the park, so he stopped to admire the flight of the homer, then after flipping his bat dramatically à la Reggie Jackson and others, he "slowly jogged around the bases." The next day, the opposing manager sent a pitcher-delivered message to Rodriguez, drilling him with a fastball in his ribs during his first trip to the plate. It had been a "Welcome to pro ball, kid" moment, and Rodriguez accepted the lesson and trotted to first base. Several weeks later, Lezcano noted with a smile that when Rodriguez hit subsequent home runs, "he's almost sprinting. I have to slow him down."[7]

Immediately, and through mid-May, his bat remained on fire; he basically outclassed and outhit the entire league. He hit .406 over that span, with a two-week zenith of .455 with 10 home runs, and he maintained a .342 batting average for the month of May to go with a jaw-dropping 13 homers and 35 runs driven in over a 31-game period. For such numbers, he was named the Mariners' Minor League Player of the Month, the first of many significant professional honors to come his way. By season's end, he also was selected as the Prospect of the Year; his grooming for a trip to the majors was coming to fruition.

Even back then, the media clamored to talk to Rodriguez, and Lezcano had to set up schedules for interviews, limiting press access so as not to overwhelm and distract the rising star. "It was hard on him, I had to set up a little break once in awhile. 'You can interview him these two days, but these two days, leave him alone.' But he was a well-rounded kid all the way and very humble and eager to learn: 'Yes, sir. No, sir.' He was a true professional from day one. He's more mature now, but he was like the same [as a] kid."

Lezcano recounted the time they went to a local batting cage where Rodriguez, the man-child, was to sign autographs. "He was having fun with the kids, and you could see the kid coming out in him."

That kid was evident the time Alex missed a bus. Lezcano recalled the time his team stopped by a restaurant for lunch, and he informed his squad when the bus would roll out. Later, thinking everyone was on board, Lezcano instructed the driver to pull out. "Alex and two other guys were not there and had to take a taxi for about 40 minutes to get to our hotel. Maybe he learned a lesson with that one. In the minor leagues you say the bus leaves at a certain time and it leaves—if you're not there, then you gotta find your own way.

"He was a normal kid. He just wanted to be treated like everybody else, not special—no less, no more." Even the Seattle organization pretty much handled him normally, giving no special instructions other than, according to Lezcano, "Just play him everyday."[8]

Before Rodriguez, sporting a .319 batting average in Class A ball, had the opportunity to play in the Midwest's All-Star contest, he climbed the ladder to Class AA, assigned to Seattle's farm club in Jacksonville, Florida. Rodriguez's flair for dramatics quickly was evident; he launched a home run in his first at bat with the Suns.[9]

THE BIG LEAGUE CALL-UP

His stay with Jacksonville was a very brief 59 at bats' worth of baseball over only 17 games. He hit a solid .288 before the call came on July 7. Mariners officials told him he was to hop a plane and report to the major-league team, catching up with them in Boston.[10] The original Mariners concept had been to keep Rodriguez with Jacksonville until they would fulfill their contractual promise with a September call-up to the majors. Needing him to fill in some at shortstop with the parent club, however, that plan evaporated.[11] They could have resorted to a different shortstop in their system but were reportedly "stunned by his rate of progress." As Lou Piniella observed before Rodriguez's big-league debut, "We were going to call him up next year anyway, and six or seven weeks of double-A ball was not going to make a huge difference."[12]

On July 8 in Boston's old but venerable Fenway Park, the one-time home of Ted Williams, the young but talented Rodriguez made his big-league opening night as the Mariners' starting shortstop, completing his meteoric climb from the halls and fields of his high school to the majors. Remarkably, at the age of 18 years, 11 months, and 11 days, he was just the third 18-year-old to take the field at the shortstop position since the modern era of baseball dawned in 1900.[13]

His mother sat in the stands with a feeling of eerie incredulity; she repeatedly asked herself, "Am I dreaming?"[14] As for Alex's incredibly swift ascension to the majors, a butterfly-ridden Rodriguez told *Sports Illustrated*, "Last year I would have paid anything to go watch a major league game. This year I'm playing in one."[15]

The following day, Rodriguez registered his first major-league hit, coming at the expense of Sergio Valdez. Rodriguez had been jammed on the pitch but was able to get wood on the ball, beating third baseman Scott Cooper's throw to the bag by a split second. Nobody present, of course, had an inkling that this game represented the start of superstardom. Still, he *was* after all, a rookie; the next game he fanned three times and committed an error but, as usual, took it all in stride.

On July 14, there was a charged atmosphere in the Pacific Northwest as the Mariner fans were anxious for the home debut of Rodriguez. His Mariners took on a team that would play a huge role in his future, the New York Yankees. Bernie Williams, the Bronx leadoff hitter, smashed a grounder up the middle, where Rodriguez was forced to dive to his left to snare the ball, trampolined to his feet à la Ozzie Smith, and made a strong throw to nip Williams. The crowd roared, and the Seattle love affair with Rodriguez had begun.[16]

Seattle spectators who returned two days later were treated to his first run batted in, coming off New York's Jimmy Key, and soon a Mariners broadcaster came up with the "A-Rod" tag for the up-and-coming star.[17]

He was joining a team rich with great hitters—Griffey Jr., Jay Buhner, and Edgar Martinez—but with only one big-name pitcher, the 6-foot, 10-inch fireballing Randy Johnson; and even Johnson could scrape together only 13 wins on this dreary season. The Mariners would go 49–63 in the so-called Mild, Mild West Division. As meager as their win total was, they finished close behind Texas, a first-place team with a pathetic 52–62 slate.

However, a players' strike ended this season at midnight on August 11. The union refused to listen to owners' demands for a salary cap and an alteration to the rules concerning arbitration in order to curtail "runaway salaries" of the day. Talks went on until September 14, when the season officially was declared dead, with no winners and, for the first time since 1904, no World Series. It was a pathetic scene: "A set of millionaires walked the golf course instead of picket lines in protest against the fiscal policies of another group of millionaires."[18]

On the year, Rodriguez logged less than a month with the Mariners, where his hitting was a bit wobbly with a batting average just over .200 with 20 strikeouts in 17 starts at shortstop. "Rival pitchers noticed he was overanxious, and they began changing speeds and throwing him breaking balls out of the strike zone. Alex could not help lunging at these pitches."[19] As a result, his average had plunged while his strikeout total soared; on August 2 he was optioned to the Triple-A Calgary Cannons, where he would spend the rest of their season, hitting .311 over some 32 contests.

Any player still on a big-league roster at the beginning of the strike was frozen there, unable to play pro ball at any level, but because Rodriguez had been sent to Calgary earlier in August, he was free to play ball there. Fortuitously, the front office had not kept him with the parent club.

This season marked the only time he would appear as a player at a level lower than Triple-A ball. For the record, as a Cannon (and a well-disciplined one, not a loose cannon) he spanked the ball (six homers, 21 RBIs) but found, for the first time, that his running game was not without flaw; he was caught stealing four times versus two successful ventures.

His total combined statistics from all four of the leagues he played in were solid: 21 home runs, 86 runs driven in, and 23 steals to go with his .300 batting average over 131 contests.[20] He had spent time with four clubs over a five-month span and had played in front of crowds in 16 states as well as in Canada. He had endured a broken nose, the introduction to life on the road, and a sip or two from the proverbial big-league "cup of coffee." He summarized, "That's a tough road. I've learned a lot about professional baseball along the way."[21]

However, Rodriguez hit just .204 over just 54 at bats at the big-league level. His big-league tenure resulted in 11 hits and just four runs and two runs driven in. For one thing, he knew he would have to cut down on his strikeouts or greatly increase his power numbers to justify high strikeout totals; he had struck out 20 times, 35 percent of his plate appearances, an alarming rate.

Not content with his endless hours of work and play through season's end, Rodriguez set off for the Dominican Republic to play in their winter league. A personal event shook Rodriguez there: During pregame work-outs there, his father, Victor, made his appearance. "I was taking batting practice," said Alex. "He just bought a ticket and came to the stadium." Naturally, Alex did not recognize his own father, but when he was informed that a spectator was, in fact, Victor, Alex was badly shaken. He later commented, "I almost broke down." After recovering his composure, the two agreed to have lunch together the following day. Alex never showed. As he would later put it, "This was my father, yes. But this was the man who walked away from my mom." He added that although he conceded his father had treated him well in the past and had been a good father, he could not ignore the fact that Victor simply vanished from his family's life and plight. "I couldn't just go and see him, just like that."[22]

In a December 2000 magazine piece, Mel Antonen wrote that over the previous 15 years Alex had seen his father only three times.[23] In 2006, Rich Hofman stated that over the last few years Alex "has [had] contact with his father. I really don't know to what extent, but the relationship has been reestablished."[24]

His 1994 stay in the winter league represented the first time he had set foot on Dominican soil since his family moved to the United States when he was eight years old. He observed that his trip there did represent more than, say, improving "the backhand play in the hole. I came to find out where I'm from."[25]

That aside, he was there primarily to work on baseball, to "try to perfect my game," and not to sightsee.[26] He especially needed work "on being more selective at the plate."[27]

Believing the brand of ball played there was the "strongest in the Caribbean," he wanted to further test himself. He joined the Escogido Leones, and in some regards he failed that litmus test, hitting a meager .179 that winter and feeling a bit out of his class, although he was slick in the field. Nevertheless, he called the "brutal" experience the most difficult one of his life to date, confiding that he "just got my tail kicked."[28] He further noted that he was "overmatched" and that his "mind really wasn't into it. I think it woke me up a little bit."[29]

The Dominican brand of baseball was indeed difficult in that there the games were held on substandard playing fields, often studded with rocks. Nor did it help that he played under the scrutiny of "often-unforgiving crowds."[30] Humbled but wiser, he returned to Florida.

It is noteworthy that while playing winter ball, Rodriguez displayed his ease in fitting in with both American and Latin players. He stated that he was among just a few players who were "comfortable with both sides." One writer said that in a few years many fans would see Rodriguez as being "the poster boy for the new era, photogenic, articulate in English and Spanish," and highly productive with the bat.[31]

ON TO THE 1995 SEASON, A YEAR OF UPS AND DOWNS

The players' strike that had caused the 1994 season to screech to an ugly halt still had not been resolved as 1995's opening day loomed near.

One publication later stated, "Faced with the prospect of seeing 'replacement players'—mostly marginally talented amateurs—take the field, the major leaguers returned to work on the eve of the scheduled opening of the season. To allow them to get into playing shape, the start was pushed back three weeks and the season shortened." Each team would play just 144 games rather than the normal 162-game schedule.[32]

Earlier, the Players' Association had made it clear that if anybody appeared in the major leagues as a replacement player, they would be viewed as a scab and would never be welcome in the union. Minor-league play was permitted to continue with very few players jumping to the majors. So, while the turmoil and logistics over the resumption of big-league play were being hashed out, Rodriguez reported to the minors.

The first appearance of Rodriguez in the official publication of the American League known as the *Red Book* featured him among the promising rookies of 1995. It mentioned the fact that he had appeared at "all four levels of the Mariners system in 1994, hitting a combined .300 (144 hits in 480 at bats) with 21 HR, 86 RBIs and 23 SB in 131 games."[33]

The first appearance of Rodriguez in a wedding dress took place in May 1995. Although he had begun the season with the Tacoma Rainiers, the Mariners new AAA team, it was not at all unusual for prospects to be shuttled the 31 miles from Tacoma to Seattle. On May 6, Rodriguez got a call up to the bigs and stayed with the Mariners for three weeks.

It was during that span that the Seattle veterans unveiled their annual rookie hazing tradition. Every year when the team prepared to fly out of Kansas City at the end of their first series there, rookies, having toweled off after their postgame shower, scurried to their lockers, where they discovered their street clothes had been whisked away and the only garb left behind was, in Rodriguez's case, a silver dress and high-heeled shoes. His only two choices were to miss the team plane, a taboo, or suit up in dress and heels. To make the tradition more unbearable, the rookies were required to sign autographs and to continue wearing the outlandish outfits throughout the flight.[34]

Although the good-natured Rodriguez could handle that humiliation, he found it more taxing when the Mariners made him into a "human yo-yo going between Tacoma and Seattle" that season. Counting his dispatch to Tacoma after spring training, four times he was shipped off by the Mariners, leaving him "drained, defeated." After being with the Mariners for some futile at bats ("he couldn't hit a breaking ball with a tennis racket"),[35] he went to Tacoma on May 27, was recalled on June 8, starting 11 games and belting his first big-league home run, a June 12 blow versus the Kansas City Royals' pitcher Tom Gordon.

It was back to Tacoma on June 23, to Seattle on July 20, and down to the bushes once more on August 15 before finally getting an August 31 callback that would, for all intents and purposes, mark the end of his minor-league days (in 1996, he would spend two more games in Tacoma on a rehab assignment after coming off the disabled list).

After his third demotion, however, his spirits had plummeted as low as his batting average (which hovered a bit above .200). "Each demotion chipped away at me," he remembered vividly. He admitted that after he learned of his last demotion, he sat, head down by his clubhouse cubicle, and wept.[36]

He phoned his mother and informed her that he was disgusted with the organization and that he was headed home. The always levelheaded Lourdes dissuaded him, first by snapping at him, telling him that if he came home he did not "have a house here." Then, more lovingly and placatingly, she bolstered him, saying, "You are going to make it!" He then realized that "quitting out of frustration" when he certainly did have the latent talent to make it would be folly.[37]

Rodriguez simply had to understand that he was behind veteran short-stops Luis Sojo and Felix Fermin on the Mariners' depth chart. When Fermin went down with an injury in early May, Rodriguez came up, but, when Fermin returned at the end of the month, a demotion followed. Later, when Sojo, who also had been playing second base, was injured, Fermin slid over to handle second and Rodriguez returned to Seattle once more. Clearly such a vagabond season was trying for the youngster.

Sojo had praise for Rodriguez saying, among other things, that Rodriguez displayed curiosity, constantly asking questions, thirsting to learn more about the game of baseball.[38] Still, those words did little to alleviate Rodriguez's discontent. He commented, "Every time I came up [to Seattle], I felt it was going to be the last time," but each time he again was sent packing, off to Tacoma, the ordeal was even more troublesome.[39]

It did help when Griffey Jr. became an informal mentor to Rodriguez. He began by insisting that A-Rod be assigned the locker next to his own. Having gone through much of what Rodriguez was experiencing, including a flash-flood-like rise to the majors as a teenager, Griffey truly could relate to the young shortstop. "He knows if he has a question about anything," said the veteran outfielder, "all he has to do is ask." Due to their bonding, some even took to calling Rodriguez "Junior Jr."[40]

At any rate, on August 20, largely due to injuries to key players such as Griffey Jr.—a broken wrist cost him almost half of the season—Seattle had languished 12.5 games behind the California Angels, but they were about to break out of their funk and put together a sizzling streak.

Led by Randy Johnson, who would win this season's Cy Young Award with an 18–2 record, Seattle made their charge. Over one stretch, they reeled off 16 victories while losing only three times. By the final day of August, just in time to be eligible for inclusion on the Mariners' postseason roster, Rodriguez was back with Seattle, experiencing their "remarkable 'Refuse to Lose' playoff run." Then, by the conclusion of the regular season, the Mariners had stormed back to tie California at 78 wins and 66 losses in the American League West Division, forcing a one-game playoff, which the Mariners won.[41]

Despite the youth of A-Rod and, for that matter, the greenness of the Mariners as a franchise as a whole, Seattle found themselves in their first postseason ever. It was true, in the overall baseball scheme of things, Seattle, a franchise born in 1976, was still, like Rodriguez, just a youngster, but their fans felt it was time to break out. Somehow their scant 79 victories, counting their playoff win over the Angels, was enough for them to win the West, up two notches from a third-place finish the previous season. It was onto the American League Division Series for the upstart Mariners.

There, Rodriguez, looking upon the pennant race and his taste of postseason play as a solid learning experience, played in just one game in the American League Division Series, going hitless in his only official trip to the plate. He told *Sports Illustrated* that going into his first postseason he fully understood his role. "I was there to pinch run or fill in if someone got hurt—and it didn't bother me at all."[42]

In that Division Series against Rodriguez's future team, the Yankees, the teams battled through five fierce games, with the Yanks capturing the first two contests, both home contests, to pile drive the Mariners into a deep, dark hole, especially after winning the emotional Game 2 in 15 innings of grind-'em-out baseball. Returning to Seattle for the next three games, however, the Mariners clawed their way out of their grave with the single-mindedness of a zombie and took three in a row, capped off by a thrilling 11-inning finale to secure the upset. In that game, Griffey Jr. propelled a record-tying playoff record with his fifth home run in the eighth, but the Yankees scratched out a run in the ninth to force extra innings, then took a 5–4 lead in the top half of the 11th. A Joey Cora bunt single opened the Mariners attack, Griffey singled him to third, and Edgar Martinez absolutely ripped a line drive down the line in left. Cora scored the tying run, and Griffey, running through third base coach Sam Perlozzo's stop sign, secured the 6–5 nail-biter.

Rodriguez later wrote that his most vivid memory of that series took place right then, in the Kingdome's on-deck circle, cheers cascading down, when Martinez stroked the ball that drove in Griffey with the winning run. The experience, that single moment of elation, led him to say quite simply, "There's nothing like winning."[43]

Rodriguez's manager, former Yankee outfielder Lou Piniella, elaborated that he felt his young shortstop had learned a great deal simply by being with the club down the stretch run, even when he was on the bench. Although the feisty, volatile Piniella clearly saw Rodriguez as his future starting shortstop, "it wouldn't have been fair to the guys on the field or to Alex [to put him in the starting lineup]."[44] Instead, Piniella felt he had to stick with his veterans.

Having survived the formidable Yankees, the Mariners advanced to take on the Cleveland Indians. Again, Rodriguez chalked up just one at bat in his only contest and left no imprint on the American League Championship Series when he fanned. Cleveland, stacked with sluggers such as Jim Thome, Manny Ramirez, and Albert Belle, still needed six games to dispatch Seattle. The frantic, exciting, gut-wrenching season was over.

For Rodriguez, it also had been a season that saw him punish the ball at Tacoma, hitting .360 over 214 at bats, complemented by 15 home runs and 45 RBIs in 54 games. He was tabbed as the Triple-A All-Star shortstop by *Baseball America* and labeled both the Best Arm and the Most Exciting Player of the Pacific Coast League by that same highly regarded publication.

With the Mariners, he managed a less-than-glorious .232 batting average with five homers and 19 RBIs. His frequent strikeouts were still an issue: 44 times in 54 minor-league games and an additional 42 over 48 big-league games, perilously close to one strikeout per game played. Another way of looking at it, 24 percent of his official at bats resulted in unproductive strikeouts.

The 1995 season "had probably saved major league baseball in Seattle." In the past, fans were not exactly plentiful at home games, and by the opening of that year, the owners began contemplating packing up the franchise and moving elsewhere. With the success of '95, the owners decided to stay and committed themselves to building a new stadium.[45] In just a few years, that facility would be Rodriguez's new home, one where he would showcase his splendid skills.

NOTES

1. Glenn Stout, *On the Field With . . . Alex Rodriguez* (New York: Little, Brown, 2002), 59.

2. Dave Aust, Pete Vanderwarker, Tim Hevly, and Bob Wickwire, eds., *1994 Seattle Mariners Information Guide* (Seattle, WA: Mariners Baseball Club, 1994), 86.

3. Alex Rodriguez and Greg Brown, *Hit a Grand Slam* (Dallas: Taylor, 1998), 30.

4. Stew Thornley, *Alex Rodriguez: Slugging Shortstop* (Minneapolis, MN: Lerner, 1998), 33.

5. Author's interview with Carlos Lezcano, July 24, 2006.

6. Mike Shalin, *Alex Rodriguez: A+ Shortstop* (Champaign, IL: Sports Publishing, 1999), 35.

7. Stout, *On the Field With . . . Alex Rodriguez*, 63–64.

8. Author's interview with Carlos Lezcano, July 24, 2006.

9. Thornley, *Alex Rodriguez: Slugging Shortstop*, 34; ibid.

10. Shalin, *Alex Rodriguez: A+ Shortstop*, 35.

11. Mark Stewart, *Alex Rodriguez: Gunning for Greatness* (Brookfield, CT: Millbrook Press, 1999), 23.

12. Stout, *On the Field With . . . Alex Rodriguez*, 68, 77.

13. The Sporting News, *The 1995 American League Red Book* (New York: The Sporting News), 46.

14. Thornley, *Alex Rodriguez: Slugging Shortstop*, 35.

15. Michael A. Pare, *Sports Stars, Series 3* (Detroit: UXL, 1970), 244.

16. Thornley, *Alex Rodriguez: Slugging Shortstop*, 35–36.

17. Stewart, *Alex Rodriguez: Gunning for Greatness*, 29.

18. David S. Neft, Richard M. Cohen, and Michael L. Neft, *The Sports Encyclopedia: Baseball*, 23rd ed. (New York: St. Martin's Press, 2003), 601.

19. Stewart, *Alex Rodriguez: Gunning for Greatness*, 24.

20. Shalin, *Alex Rodriguez: A + Shortstop*, 33.

21. Ken Rappoport, *Super Sports Star Alex Rodriguez* (Berkeley Heights, NJ: Enslow, 2004), 21.

22. Shalin, *Alex Rodriguez: A + Shortstop*, 17–18.

23. Mel Antonen, "Alex Rodriguez: Master of Baseball Arts," *Baseball Digest*, December 2000, 61.

24. Author's interview with Rich Hofman, May 3, 2006.

25. Rappoport, *Super Sports Star*, 23.

26. Thornley, *Alex Rodriguez: Slugging Shortstop*, 37.

27. Kim Covert, *Alex Rodriguez* (Mankato, MN: Capstone Press, 2002), 22.

28. Thornley, *Alex Rodriguez: Slugging Shortstop*, 37.

29. Stout, *On the Field With . . . Alex Rodriguez*, 85.

30. Michael Bradley, *Alex Rodriguez* (Tarrytown, NY: Benchmark Books, 2005), 20.

31. Tim Wendel, *The New Face of Baseball: The 100-Year Rise and Triumph of Latinos in America's Favorite Sport* (New York: HarperCollins, 2003), 198–99.

32. Neft, Cohen, and Neft, *The Sports Encyclopedia: Baseball*, 23rd ed., 609.

33. The Sporting News, *The 1995 American League Red Book*, 46.

34. Rodriguez and Brown, *Hit a Grand Slam*, 32.

35. Anonymously quoting a big-league manager, Stout, *On the Field With . . . Alex Rodriguez*, 88.

36. Jim Gallagher, *Alex Rodriguez: Latinos in Baseball* (Childs, MD: Mitchell Lane, 2000), 29.

37. Rodriguez and Brown, *Hit a Grand Slam*, 32–33.

38. Wendel, *The New Face of Baseball*, 193.

39. Thornley, *Alex Rodriguez: Slugging Shortstop*, 42–43.

40. Ibid., 40.

41. Rodriguez and Brown, *Hit a Grand Slam*, 33.
42. Pare, *Sports Stars*, 245.
43. Rodriguez and Brown, *Hit a Grand Slam*, 33.
44. Bradley, *Alex Rodriguez*, 22–23.
45. Gallagher, *Alex Rodriguez: Latinos in Baseball*, 33.

Chapter 4

SO GOOD, SO YOUNG,
1996–1998

The 1996 campaign was to be Rodriguez's first full season in the majors, and he was still, at the age of 20, very young. He was also still an unproven hitter, carrying a meager .224 lifetime average into the season. Nevertheless, by as early as that year's spring training camp, he felt that he had "an understanding of what's going on. This is not like my first spring—that I'm in awe of the big leagues or something." Instead, he said, he was simply "trying to get my stuff together."[1] By the summertime, Cal Ripken Jr. would call him "a special player" who somehow was "doing it like he has been in the league four or five years."[2]

Rodriguez, having worked out with a personal trainer throughout the winter back home in Miami and having adhered to a diet set up by a nutritionist, reported to camp in the best shape he had ever achieved.[3] He then sought out advice on hitting from teammate Edgar Martinez, the reigning American League batting title winner, and worked out rigorously with his double-play mate, Joey Cora, focusing on turning two. In the meantime, Rodriguez scalded the ball during exhibition games, boasting a .344 batting average as if to demonstrate he had nothing left to prove.

At one point during spring training, Rodriguez strode purposefully to Lou Piniella and told his skipper, "I'm ready." Piniella nodded, "I know you are, son," and basically, with that nod, gave him the shortstop job right then and there.[4]

Just seven years earlier, Ken Griffey Jr. made his major-league debut with the Mariners; now Seattle was to be blessed with two dynamic young studs. Coming off their playoff appearance in 1995, optimism was in the crisp Pacific Northwest air.

Even when Rodriguez first came up to the big club, Piniella had commented that a manager can tell when a young player is tentative, "The kid who is scared sits at the end of the bench." With Rodriguez, however, it was a different scenario. When Piniella looked down his bench, ready to bring a sub into the game, he "always became highly visible. He would grab a bat or his glove." He was acting not unlike a star basketball performer, a Larry Bird who, when the game is on the line, craves and even demands the ball to be in his hands.[5]

Seattle batting coach Lee Elia loved Rodriguez's bat speed, quickness, and hitting mechanics. Elia gushed that though he had worked with future Hall of Famers Mike Schmidt, Ryne Sandberg, and Don Mattingly, he had not "seen too many guys who can get their bat through the hitting zone any faster than Alex. With his ability, there's no telling what he can accomplish."[6]

He believed Rodriguez's quickness gave him the ability to handle searing fastballs and his sound mechanics allowed him to hit all other offerings. Still, Elia believed Rodriguez's swing was too long and would require some retooling. Elia also contended his student would have better bat control if they changed his grip on the bat. He had been holding his pinkie finger over the knob of the bat—not, as Jerry Seinfeld would say, that there was anything wrong with that (Willie Stargell and others used such a grip to provide a tad more leverage for his swing)—but Elia wanted Rodriguez to shoot for more bat control rather than sheer power. The veteran instructor also "squared him up [to the plate]" and told him to strive to simply place the ball, to go with the pitch, and to try to drill line drives.[7]

Incidentally, Rodriguez continued to be a loyal friend and son. Throughout the season, he constantly kept in touch with "his high school buddies and his mother," racking up telephone bills as whopping as $650 per month.[8]

Rodriguez was indeed a very apt pupil and began studying videotape, much like Tony Gwynn, focusing on teammate Edgar Martinez. As A-Rod put it, "When you're with the best, you learn from the best."[9] He frequently scrutinized tapes that ran three hours and contained all of Martinez's hits from 1994 and 1995, when Martinez led the league in hitting with an ostentatious .356 average.[10]

It paid off. Fellow videophile Gwynn noticed Rodriguez hitting in the batting cage during spring training and admired how he kept his hands inside the ball, how he would foul off pitches he could not handle easily, and how he could "inside-out" his swing when needed. Gwynn predicted a big year for the up-and-coming hitter.[11]

THE BIG BREAKTHROUGH SEASON

He began the season hitting ninth in the batting order, but an unperturbed Rodriguez told the *Everett Washington Daily Herald,* "The first thing I've got to understand is my role on this team. If my role is to play good defense or to be a contact hitter or to hit home runs or to bunt, whatever I have to do, then that's my role."[12]

A little earlier that year, Rodriguez had spied an article quoting a coach who said the team would be content if he played his position well and hit only .250 in 1996. He quickly snipped the article out and used it for motivation. By year's end, he had made the coach's low expectations appear foolish.[13]

In fact, he did quite well soon after some right-out-of-the-gate tribulations, and some pointed to his 12th-inning, game-winning hit on 1996's opening day as foreshadowing his upcoming dazzling success. Soon Seattle strung together an eight-game winning streak, jumping into first place in the American League West. In a sport in which, as any sandlotter can recite with ease, "Pitching is the name of the game," the Mariners were in contention due to their inferno-hot hitting.

A pulled hamstring muscle sent him to the disabled list on April 22. After his recovery, he still felt hampered and stated that he had played the bulk of the season "at 85 percent."[14]

The day after he came off his rehab, on May 7, Seattle skipper Lou Piniella decided to move Rodriguez, then hitting .279, to the number two hole in the batting order, directly in front of Griffey Jr., hoping he would get on base often to set the table for the slugging Griffey Jr. as well as Edgar Martinez and Jay Buhner, who followed him at the plate. Writer Michael A. Pare commented, "The move turned Rodriguez's season around."[15] The experiment was a challenge at first, but one that came with a definite upside: Pitchers would challenge Rodriguez, often with fastballs, not wishing to walk him, subsequently having to face the veteran big sticks. Rodriguez succinctly summed up the situation, "The most obvious thing Junior [Griffey] does for me is get me better pitches."[16]

He immediately made those pitchers pay, his bat a lethal weapon. He pasted the ball to the tune of .367 the rest of the way, giving him an overall batting average of .358, the highest ever for a player 21 years old or younger. Additionally, only Lloyd Waner, with 223 hits in 1927, had more than Rodriguez's 215 for a man 21 or younger; only Rodriguez, Joe

Cronin, and Vern Stephens had scored and driven in 120 runs as big-league shortstops.

In May, Rodriguez faced Baltimore's Scott Erickson, and when the Orioles hurler attempted to sneak a high fastball by him, A-Rod sent the ball over the left-field fence for his first major-league grand slam, to bust a tie game wide open. Two more would follow that year, allowing him to lead the majors in slams.

A-Rod's power numbers also soared; he enjoyed his first multi-home-run game shortly after moving up in the lineup and followed up that with a game in which he smacked a grand slam and amassed six runs driven in. Clearly he possessed "light tower power," having the ability to hit 'em high, hard, deep—and, for that matter, often. After 63 contests, he was averaging nearly one run driven in per game. Not long after that, his face appeared on the cover of *Sports Illustrated*. He had arrived and had yet to reach the age of 21. In an interesting coincidence, Rodriguez slammed his 21st home run of the season on his 21st birthday.[17]

A-Rod made the American League All-Star team as the league's leading hitter and, as a newcomer to the event, anxiously suited up, as the backup to his hero Cal Ripken Jr. He became the youngest shortstop to appear in an All-Star Game and the 15th-youngest player ever to see All-Star play.[18]

Although he conceded that he was excited, he stated he was not surprised at being there. He went 0 for 1 with the entire All-Star weekend's events blending into "a blur." His first All-Star hit would have to wait until the following season's midsummer showcase.[19]

If A-Rod was smoldering hot by the end of July—and he most certainly was after hitting .383 for the month—in August, he was a five-alarm conflagration. Twice he took American League Player of the Week honors and breezed to claim the Player of the Month Award. In 29 games that month, he starched the ball to a .435 clip, launched nine home runs, drove in 28 runs, and crossed home 30 times. From August 16 to September 4, he rained down hits all over the park, compiling a career-high 20-game hitting streak, good for a .457 average. His 54 hits in August represented the most by a player in a single month since 1980.[20]

Personal success, Rodriguez understood, did not necessarily equate to team success. The Mariners did get fine showings from their mini-Murderers' Row with Griffey Jr. (49 HR), Jay Buhner (44 HR), Edgar Martinez (26 HR), Paul Sorrento (23 HR), and Dan Wilson (18 HR); however, the team lacked pitching, recording only four complete games, and an injured Randy Johnson could supply only five victories. Their two top winners, Sterling Hitchcock and Bob Wells, combined for just 25 wins, one less than Johnson's eventual season high. Piniella was forced to go through pitchers at a distressing rate, employing nearly 30 on the year.

Seattle did hang around as a contender for most of the season, but they came up short. They finished the year four-and-a-half games in arrears of the Texas Rangers, winners of 90 games. The Mariners, who had not enjoyed a winning season prior to 1991, would up with just their third year playing above .500 ball.

By this time, Rodriguez was entrenched as a heartthrob, a term usually associated with rock and movie stars. He frequently was inundated with squeals from adoring fans "as soon as he poked his head out of the dugout." When he disclosed the fact that he had not attended his high school prom, he received a slew of invitations from naive girls.[21]

Over the winter, Rodriguez could look back on his offensive spree with pride. No American League right-handed batter since 1939 had hit as high as Rodriguez: .358, third highest ever for a shortstop and the loftiest ever, by eight points over Ty Cobb from way back in 1907, for a player who began the season younger than 21 years of age. A-Rod became the first American League shortstop to win a batting crown since Cleveland's Lou Boudreau turned the trick in 1944. Also, at the age of 21 years, 1 month, he became the third-youngest player to win the league's batting crown; only 20-year-olds Cobb and Al Kaline had been younger.

A-Rod's 215 hits on the year represented the most ever notched by a big-league shortstop and the second-most hits in the league that season. Rodriguez's league-leading 141 runs scored were the most in a season by a shortstop. He led the league in total bases, tying Cubs great Ernie Banks for the most total bases by a shortstop in a year, 379, a total A-Rod later would surpass four times. His sensational total of 54 doubles, also tops in the league, was the most ever by a shortstop over a big-league season, just as his .631 slugging percentage and his 91 extra base hits were bests for that position. He was redefining the position.

Toss in his 123 RBIs along with his 36 home runs, including a league-topping three grand slams, and it was quite transparent that he had constructed a monster season, one to rank among the most noteworthy in baseball history. In addition, his work with the leather was impressive enough to finish second in the league for the Gold Glove Award. Incredibly, he managed all these feats in just his first full season in the majors.

This was also the season when Rodriguez had absolutely crushed a ball 440 feet to center in spacious Tiger Stadium, and he became just the 10th man since 1976 to reach what is known as the "black seats" at Yankee

Stadium, a 416-foot shot to center. He also added a 450 footer to his résumé when he annihilated a pitch that flew seemingly endlessly before ricocheting off a distant restaurant sitting high up in Toronto's Skydome.

By the time the infield dust of the season had settled, Seattle teammate Edgar Martinez marveled, "We knew Alex had a lot of potential, but I didn't think people were expecting all this."[22]

THE MEDIA AND THE MVP

A blow to his pride came when the year's major awards were announced early in the off-season. In balloting that wound up tighter than the hinges of a new catcher's mitt, Juan Gonzalez of the Texas Rangers edged A-Rod for the MVP Award, 290 votes to 287, making this the closest race for the MVP in 36 years and one of the six-closest finishes ever.[23] Had he won, he would have been the youngest MVP recipient ever.

Rodriguez confided that he would have rather lost by 100 points than three, adding that the loss was a stinging one. What was the most baffling aspect of the defeat, though, was the fact that both Seattle members of the Baseball Writers Association of America, who select major postseason awards, penciled in Griffey (.303, 140 RBIs) as their number one selection for the MVP, and one of them, almost patronizingly, placed Rodriguez seventh, costing him the trophy. Author Dan Schlossberg wrote, "Had either of the two Seattle voters placed him on their 1996 Most Valuable Player ballots [at the number one slot], Seattle shortstop Alex Rodriguez would have beaten out Texas outfielder Juan Gonzalez. But, Bob Finnigan and Jim Street placed Rodriguez third and fourth respectively."[24] Rodriguez philosophically stated, "It was a bad year to have a great year."[25]

Still, he also said, "It hurts not to get a first-place vote from my own town after the season that I had, and that seventh-place vote killed me." Rodriguez basically felt shunned, snubbed, and worse, torpedoed by the men who covered the Mariners on a daily basis. How, he wondered, could they have listed him so low?[26]

Texas announcer Tom Grieve said of A-Rod's relationship with the media: "He loves to talk baseball, but there are so many demands on his time. He's comfortable around us, and if we have a conversation with him, he's very gracious and takes time to do that."

Grieve candidly added, some writers "don't like him. There are writers here in Texas that didn't like Alex and [some] that really liked him. My observation was Alex was always up front and available to the media even though, for whatever reason, some of them didn't like him."[27]

Seattle Times sportswriter Bob Finnigan discounted A-Rod's impact when he voted, based upon comments from a locker room interview in early September 1996 when Rodriguez told Finnigan, referring to Griffey Jr., "How can I be MVP of the American League when I'm not even MVP in our own clubhouse?"[28]

When asked if his self-deprecating remarks had hurt his MVP chances, Rodriguez replied, "If I can lose the MVP every year because of my humility, I will lose it every year." He went on to say he played baseball mainly for the "respect of the people in the clubhouse, and that includes the beat writers. When not even one of them thought you were the MVP of the team, that hurts me."[29]

"Either one of them could've been MVP," said Tom Grieve. "A lot of people thought it should have been Alex and he was asked at the end of the season who he thought should be MVP and he said he thought Griffey should. That was the politically correct answer, but deep down inside, no player feels that way. When you're that kind of a player having that kind of a year, you say to yourself, 'I am the MVP. I should be the MVP.' He deferred to the other player who was the veteran player on the team.

"Now, I don't know that Alex ever created any kind of controversy, but Gonzalez won the award. I don't know that there was anything on record where Alex was at all bitter about that. I think if you ask him with a lie detector if he was upset about that, the answer probably comes out, 'Yes.' But, heck, I don't blame him; I would have felt the same way."[30]

"He should have five MVPs—they took away at least two or three," opined Eddie Rodriguez. "A lot of people said it was because he was too perfect, 'I don't vote for him because he's too perfect, too good.' You know, a lot of times the sportswriters haven't been in the trenches; they write because they have to write, they haven't been [there]."[31]

Rodriguez was named *The Sporting News* Player of the Year, winning by an avalanche of votes by his peers in both leagues. That only could serve as a slight consolation for his not having garnered the grandfather of awards, the MVP trophy.

Mark McGwire paid tribute to what Rodriguez had accomplished, calling his season "unbelievable," and stating that a friend of his on the professional golf tour compared A-Rod to Tiger Woods as men who "come along like this every 10 to 15 years or so."[32]

Griffey had one fear regarding Rodriguez's breakout season, "I just hope people don't expect him to put up those same numbers every year. I hope that they're not going to say he's had a bad year if he hits .330 with 25 homers and 90 RBI." Griffey fretted that Rodriguez might then feel as if he had to put up monumental numbers annually in order to feel as if he had a Rodriguez-worthy season. Such fears would prove to be groundless.[33]

After the season was through, he was invited to be a part of an All-Star team that was to make a trip to Japan to play a series of games against their stars. At first, he considered resting for next season, but the prospect of playing with Cal Ripken Jr. was too appealing to pass up. He found the experience to be rewarding in that he learned so much from Ripken, both about the game they both cherished so much—mainly about respecting the game—and about life in general. He commented that Ripken was "everything he thought he would be."[34]

When he returned to his home in Florida, he handed over $25,000 to one Miami unit of the Boys and Girls Clubs so they could build a new baseball field. Eddie Rodriguez, his former coach, was overwhelmed. Never before, he said, had a former player returned there and been generous like Rodriguez. "Alex just did it. 'Whatever you need,' he said."[35]

When some critics said Rodriguez had probably just experienced a somewhat fluky peak year, that he never again could match such heights, he took that as a personal affront. He commented, "I love it when they say that was a career year for me. That's a challenge to me, a major challenge."[36]

Lou Piniella looked back over A-Rod's superlative 1996 showing and stated, "It's no fluke. The kid can play. He's the real McCoy. Baseball-wise, he's way above his years. He may not have a year like that again, but he's going to have some good ones."[37]

Because A-Rod had stunned the baseball world with his myriad records so rapidly in his career, in his first complete season, author Ken Rappoport mused, "What was next?"[38]

WHAT CAME NEXT

In 1997, while most of the country shuddered in the frostiness of the short, bitter days of February, Rodriguez was reporting early for spring training workouts. He felt it necessary to put in about two weeks' worth of work on his defense to "get his rhythm back."[39]

Coming off the remarkable season he had just enjoyed, virtually everyone was employing hyperbole to describe Rodriguez. Only, as it would turn out, they were not really guilty of exaggeration because he was every bit as talented as he had displayed. Ernie Banks shook his head in amazement, saying, "Alex Rodriguez is going to do things I never came close to doing." Although he said he did not want to place additional pressure on the young star, "he's going to set a new standard for shortstops." Yet another former shortstop, Alan Trammell, chipped in, "Let's be honest. The year he had could be the best a shortstop has ever had."[40]

When June rolled around, Rodriguez enjoyed a 16-game hitting streak in which he hit .343, 15 points *lower* than he would hit for the entire month. On June 5, when Seattle had made their way to Detroit to face the Tigers and pitcher Felipe Lira, Rodriguez clicked. In his first at bat, he pounded a delivery deep to right-center field, and his next plate appearance yielded a routine single. After making an out in the sixth inning, he connected for a blast over center fielder Brian Hunter. By the time the ball rattled around spacious Tiger Stadium, A-Rod cruised into third with a triple. By his final trip to the plate, the game was a laugher; the Mariners had scored 14 times. Needing a double to hit for the cycle for his first time, Rodriguez looped a Doug Brocail fastball into shallow right field, just inside the foul line, and he easily coasted into second.[41]

Interestingly, that night a Seattle company was running a radio contest as a promotion: If a player hit for the cycle, a prize of $1 million would be awarded to a fan. Rodriguez later joked, "I can't wait to get home and get my cut."[42]

June was also the month the Mariners bolted into first place, despite having to place Rodriguez on the disabled list for a portion of their torrid stretch. Rodriguez was injured when he tried to score on a wild pitch. He collided with pitcher Roger Clemens, who was covering the plate, and wound up sitting out 14 games (from June 12 to 27), only to return in a big way, homering off Anaheim's Chuck Finley in his first at bat back with his teammates.

Such a power outburst was common on the 1997 Mariners as they were swatting "home runs in records numbers." In all, they hoisted 264 homers to set the all-time record for a major-league club, with six men connecting for 20 or more long balls.[43] Griffey Jr., with 56 homers, supplied the bulk of the long balls, Paul Sorrento chipped in with 31, and Russ Davis was good for 20 in 118 games. The reliable Jay Buhner added 40; Edgar Martinez, known more for his ability to hit for average, hit 28; and 23 additional home runs, a fine total for a shortstop but 13 off his pace from the previous year, were supplied by the 21-year-old Rodriguez.

To be fair, it would have been nearly impossible for Rodriguez to match his lustrous numbers from 1996. Even with that in mind, it was difficult to find fault with a middle infielder who hit .300, slashed out 40 doubles, stole 29 bases, scored 100 times, and drove in nearly as many (84). Therefore, any charges of him falling victim to a sophomore jinx seem ill founded and petty.

On the pitching side of the slate, Randy Johnson, who went 5–0 the year before only to have the rest of the season wiped out after its first five weeks, "was nearly unbeatable, but the same could not be said for the Mariner's bullpen. Seattle's arsonists masquerading as relievers made for high-scoring games."[44]

By midsummer, Rodriguez was on the All-Star squad, elected by the fans as the starting shortstop. Under the lights of Jacobs Field in Cleveland, he collected his first midsummer classic hit, a single off Greg Maddux in his first at bat of the night.

Right after the All-Star break, Rodriguez posted a perfect four-for-four night against Texas, helping Seattle open up a four-and-a-half-game lead over the Anaheim Angels. It was his third four-hit game of the season. The Angels stomped back, however, pushing the Mariners out of first early in August. From there, it was a dogfight of World War I proportions. Finally, in September, Seattle reestablished themselves, moving into a fairly comfortable lead. They stayed perched atop the American League West, winding up six games in front of Anaheim.

Once more, Seattle broke their team record for the most wins in a season, capturing 90 victories, and aided greatly by their first month with 20 wins. In July, A-Rod and company had blazed the way to a 20–7 mark, good for a .741 win-loss percentage. Naturally, they could not maintain a winning pace anywhere near that, but they did wind up at .556, good enough to push them into the American League Division Series. They had made it to the playoffs twice over the last three years.

In just the franchise's second playoff ever, they faced the Baltimore Orioles, who won the opening two games in Seattle by identical 9–3 scores, dropped Game 3, and then clinched it all in a Mike Mussina versus Randy Johnson 3–1 duel, despite a 13-strikeout performance by "The Big Unit" (Johnson). A-Rod hit at a .313 clip on five hits, including his first postseason home run, over the four-game set, with a double and his towering solo shot off Mussina among his five hits. Nobody in the series topped his nine total bases. Still, he did whiff five times.[45]

After Mussina scattered three solo homers, representing the Mariners only runs in the opener, the triumvirate of Griffey Jr. (who soon would be named the MVP), hitting an anemic .133, Buhner, and Martinez went cold, combining to hit .182, a tad below Seattle's .218 as a team. Rodriguez commented, "This takes the sweetness out of everything."[46] Ripken Jr., cheap-pistol hot, led all hitters with his .438 batting average; the Orioles breezed into the next round of play.

It was around this season that trouble began bubbling in Seattle. First, Johnson was disgruntled and demanded a trade. Second, resentment began to crop up between Griffey and Rodriguez. Griffey allegedly "felt threatened by Rodriguez's own emergence." Griffey, in what could be construed as a direct reference to Rodriguez, told *Sport* magazine that he was not concerned when others received their "share of the spotlight." However, he went on to say that when "they get more than their share, then they say about me, 'You're not the star of this team.' But I'm the guy who has to take responsibility." He felt when the team failed, he was smacked with the ponderous weight of blame, but he never got his proper credit otherwise. Rodriguez, meanwhile, felt that although Griffey surely deserved klieg-light attention, he, too, had merited the accolades he received. He was offended by the words of the "Kid."[47]

One source went so far as to say that, by 1999, Griffey's "uneasy alliance with Alex Rodriguez had turned him paranoid as he brooded that A-Rod was usurping his grip on the team and the town." Griffey eventually would call Rodriguez "calculating" and "manipulative."[48] In short, Griffey was as unhappy as a caged canary in a coal mine.

Later, by the way, Griffey would deny that there ever had been a rift between them, comparing their relationship to that of a big brother with his younger sibling.[49]

Playing in 141 contests, Rodriguez posted 40 two-baggers and hit .300 on the button but had, for him, the low totals of 23 homers and 84 RBIs. Aside from this anomaly of a season, he would never hit fewer than 35 home runs or drive in fewer than 106 again (through 2006).

At any rate, over the off-season Rodriguez limited his attention to some charity work but mainly devoted his time to the two areas of his game that most needed attention: his fielding, far from flawless, as evidenced by his 24 errors, a personal high he would match in 2006 at third base, and his strikeouts, as he still was fanning too often for a shortstop based on the traditional view of that position (203 times from 1996 to 1997).

Around this time, it was apparent that Rodriguez was a high-profile player who was starting to get exposure via commercials, ranging from a spot on a well-known campaign for milk to endorsements of video games. His handsome face had become ubiquitous, yet he remained focused. He said his goal was baseball, not Hollywood or any other similar aspirations. He insisted that the companies he worked with, such as Nike, not only would pay him but also would contribute to good causes, such as building Little League fields in both Miami and Seattle.[50]

Clearly, the indefatigable Rodriguez did not shut it down after season's end, as he also took on a personal trainer, the same man who had trained NBA great Michael Jordan. They settled into a regimen that included workouts five or six times each week.[51]

1998: RODRIGUEZ REBOUNDS TO GREATNESS

In January 1998, two personal events of note occurred: Rodriguez began taking his first college courses, saying he was determined to eventually earn a degree. On the negative side, his house was broken into by burglars who made off with approximately $100,000 worth of cash and personal belongings. Upset by this, he put the house up for sale and settled into an apartment in Seattle.[52]

Thanks to his off-season toil, he began the season eight pounds lighter but with more strength and flexibility. He immediately got off to a great start, managing to tie a 71-year-old league record when he racked eight extra-base hits over three games from April 18 to 20. By June, he owned two hitting streaks of 13 games in length.[53] One-third of the way into the year, he had piled up 20 home runs.

About this time, a *Baseball Digest* poll listed Rodriguez as having the best arm of any big-league infielder and as being the second-most-exciting player in the game, trailing only Ken Griffey Sr.[54]

There was no question that Rodriguez would be among the 1998 All-Stars, but he went one step farther when he became the first American League player not named Cal Ripken Jr. to start at the shortstop position in more than a decade. Ripken's stranglehold came to an end when, due to his advancing age, his Baltimore Orioles shifted him to the less demanding role of third baseman. Incidentally, just months later, in September, Ripken's iron man streak ground to a halt with a terminus of 2,632 consecutive games played. In the All-Star affair, A-Rod turned in a fine performance, going two for three with his first homer in a midsummer classic.

He tagged his 30th home run of the year on July 19 and on July 31 secured his membership in the 30-30 Club when he stole his 30th base. He added a hitting skein of a dozen games from July 30 to August 12, the day he duplicated his personal high of 36 homers. He even threw in a five-for-five hitting display on August 18.[55]

Overall, however, the season turned out to be a gloomy one for him and the Mariners. The Mariners disposed of Randy Johnson in a July swap with the Houston Astros, a trade intended to help Seattle retool, not a good sign for Rodriguez, hoping to play for a winner.

There were, as always, shining moments for Rodriguez, though. On September 5, versus the Orioles, he pilfered his 40th base of the year, running successfully on the second offering to Griffey Jr. after A-Rod's fifth-inning base hit. Exactly two weeks later, he got a high, juicy fastball on a three-and-one count from the Angels' Jack McDowell. He ripped it to right field, a poke of about 390 feet, for his 40th homer, breaking a 12-day home-run drought during which he was pressing. As only the third player (and the youngest) ever to hit 40 or more homers with 40 or more stolen bases, he told the gathered media that he was constantly striving "to do things when they count and they're significant in the game. Sure, this feels good. It's something I want to accomplish."[56]

After Rodriguez blasted his 40th home run, teammate David Segui told the *Seattle Post-Intelligencer*, "It pretty much reinforces to me that he's the best player in the game. Definitely Bonds and Junior [Griffey] are right up there with him, but the way he plays the game sets him apart from everyone else, I think. He plays the game with the intensity of a fringe player." He added that he meant that in a positive way, well aware that many marginal players exert more energy and determination than some established stars. Segui added, "Most superstars wouldn't do the things that he does."[57] Around this same time, Edgar Martinez called Rodriguez the kind of youngster "you build an organization around."[58]

Six years before Rodriguez was born, Boston's Rico Petrocelli set a new American League record for home runs in a season by a shortstop with 40. Three days after connecting for his 40th, Rodriguez eclipsed Petrocelli's output, propelling a pitch from Oakland rookie Jay Witasick deep into the night.

Overall, frustration slapped A-Rod squarely; he was not content to see a once-proud team, strong contenders and/or winners over his previous three seasons, which represented virtually all of his days as a major leaguer, backpedal to square one. He regretted being in a situation he said he had never before experienced, not even back in his high school days. The Mariners were scuttled, sinking to third place, 11.5 games out of first place with a 76–85 ledger. Their top fireman, Mike Timlin, had only 19 saves. The man who considered baseball to be his entire life detested losing and the queasy feeling the accompanying impotence brought on.

This season marked the second of three times he would compile more than 200 hits; his 213 not only led the league but also ranked number six for safeties in a season by a shortstop. His game was well rounded as he hit .310 with power, 35 doubles, and 42 home runs to go with the 124 RBIs he sported, and he ran the bases well, scoring 123 times. He also displayed his durability, leading the league in at bats (686) while playing in all 161 of the Mariners games.

Further, in the field he accepted 731 total chances (104 more than he had the year before), displaying wide range while cutting his errors by one-fourth, from 24 down to 18. Alan Trammell said that a rule of thumb for the acceptable number of errors a shortstop should commit per season is about one per every 10 games started. Rodriguez's error total was not only acceptable but, given his age, was also a total that was destined to drop lower with the coming years; he never committed more than 18 again until 2006. In 2000 and 2002, he would commit just 10 errors, and he would take his defense to a career-low 8 errors in 2003, good for his finest season at short based on fielding percentage (.989).

All in all, perhaps his most eye-popping accomplishment of 1998 was his final power-plus-running combination of 42 home runs coupled with his 46 stolen bases, the most ever for a player with 40 or more homers. Although he would then go on to post five consecutive 40-home-run seasons, this was to be the only time he topped 40 stolen bases.

Rodriguez attributed his success in 1998 to his diligence, saying, "It's just a great lesson for me as a young player about the necessity of hard work." He said he was extremely proud of what he had done and would never forget this standout season. Clearly, no one would.[59]

USA Today Baseball Weekly included Rodriguez in their list of the Top 10 Madison Avenue–type ballplayers, the men who command the most commercial "earning power" and "other off-the-field marketing opportunities." Griffey Jr. was ranked number four on the list, and A-Rod checked in at number nine.[60]

As an odd sidelight to the season, Rodriguez coaxed only 45 walks all year long. Oddly, considering the threat to opponents he clearly represented, he tied Roger Maris (in 1961 when he hit 61 home runs) for having drawn the fewest intentional walks by a player with 40+ homers in a year: *zero*. Additionally, in 1999, when he would again smack 42 homers, he earned a mere two intentional passes; from his big-league debut through 1999 he would own just four such walks. "Generally speaking," said Tom Grieve, "when a player like Alex doesn't get walked intentionally, it's out of respect to the people coming up behind him."[61]

Brad Wilkerson agreed, "The talent of that ball club and the fact that, back then, he stole base a lot more than he does now, he ran a lot better, and overall you don't want to put him on base cause he'll steal second like that and be in scoring position before you know it."[62]

Clearly, the young sensation was an established threat with a wide-open, glowing future ahead.

NOTES

1. Mike Shalin, *Alex Rodriguez: A+ Shortstop* (Champaign, IL: Sports Publishing, 1999), 45.

2. David Nemec and Saul Wisnia, *100 Years of Baseball* (Lincolnwood, IL: Publications International, 2002), 493.

3. Glenn Stout, *On the Field With . . . Alex Rodriguez* (New York: Little, Brown, 2002), 92–93.

4. Widely related story.

5. Stout, *On the Field With . . . Alex Rodriguez*, 71.

6. Jim Gallagher, *Alex Rodriguez: Latinos in Baseball* (Childs, MD: Mitchell Lane, 2000), 6–7.

7. Shalin, *Alex Rodriguez: A + Shortstop*, 45, 61.

8. Wayne Lockwood, "Mariners' Alex Rodriguez: Standing Tall at Short," *Baseball Digest*, July 1997, 40.

9. Shalin, *Alex Rodriguez: A+ Shortstop*, 47.

10. Gallagher, *Alex Rodriguez: Latinos in Baseball*, 34.

11. Ibid., 34–35.

12. Michael A. Pare, *Sports Stars, Series 3* (Detroit: UXL, 1970), 245.

13. Stew Thornley, *Alex Rodriguez: Slugging Shortstop* (Minneapolis, MN: Lerner, 1998), 47.

14. Mark Stewart, *Alex Rodriguez: Gunning for Greatness* (Brookfield, CT: Millbrook Press, 1999), 29.

15. Pare, *Sports Stars*, 245.

16. Ibid., 245–46.

17. Thornley, *Alex Rodriguez: Slugging Shortstop*, 47–49.

18. Shalin, *Alex Rodriguez: A+ Shortstop*, 53.

19. Alex Rodriguez and Greg Brown, *Hit a Grand Slam* (Dallas: Taylor, 1998), 34.

20. Gallagher, *Alex Rodriguez: Latinos in Baseball*, 37.

21. Stout, *On the Field With . . . Alex Rodriguez*, 96–97.

22. Stewart, *Alex Rodriguez: Gunning for Greatness*, 30–31.

23. Dan Schlossberg, *The Baseball Almanac* (Chicago: Triumph Books, 2002), 139.

24. Ibid.

25. Stewart, *Alex Rodriguez: Gunning for Greatness*, 32.

26. Shalin, *Alex Rodriguez: A+ Shortstop*, 52.

27. Author's interview with Tom Grieve, March 8, 2006.

28. Widely quoted.

29. Gallagher, *Alex Rodriguez: Latinos in Baseball*, 38.

30. Author's interview with Tom Grieve, March 8, 2006.

31. Author's interview with Eddie Rodriguez, July 6, 2006.

32. Shalin, *Alex Rodriguez: A+ Shortstop*, 61.

33. Lockwood, "Mariners' Alex Rodriguez," 38.

34. Stout, *On the Field With . . . Alex Rodriguez*, 98–99.

35. Gallagher, *Alex Rodriguez: Latinos in Baseball*, 40–41.

36. Ibid., 8.

37. Lockwood, "Mariners' Alex Rodriguez," 38.

38. Ken Rappoport, *Super Sports Star Alex Rodriguez* (Berkeley Heights, NJ: Enslow, 2004), 26.

39. Thornley, *Alex Rodriguez: Slugging Shortstop*, 53.

40. Michael Bradley, *Alex Rodriguez* (Tarrytown, NY: Benchmark Books, 2005), 25.

41. Thornley, *Alex Rodriguez: Slugging Shortstop*, 7–9.

42. Ibid.

43. David S. Neft, Richard M. Cohen, and Michael L. Neft, *The Sports Encyclopedia: Baseball*, 23rd ed. (New York: St. Martin's Press, 2003), 631.

44. Ibid.

45. Glen Macnow, *Sports Great, Alex Rodriguez* (Berkeley Heights, NJ: Enslow, 2002), 43.

46. Bill Koenig, "Early Exit Leaves Mariners with Sour Taste," *USA Today Baseball Weekly*, October 8–14, 1997, 40.

47. Gallagher, *Alex Rodriguez: Latinos in Baseball*, 48.

48. Mark Ribowsky, *The Complete History of the Home Run* (New York: Kensington, 2003), 313.

49. Ibid., 59.

50. Macnow, *Sports Great, Alex Rodriguez*, 44.

51. Steve Riach, *Heart of a Champion: Profiles in Character,* with John Humphrey (Nashville, TN: Broadman and Holman, 2001), 18.

52. Gallagher, *Alex Rodriguez: Latinos in Baseball*, 50.

53. Ibid.

54. "Players with the Best Skills," *Baseball Digest*, August 1998, 50.

55. Gallagher, *Alex Rodriguez: Latinos in Baseball*, 52.

56. Kim Covert, *Alex Rodriguez* (Mankato, MN: Capstone Press, 2002), 6.

57. Tyler Kepner, "Alex Rodriguez's Talent Has No Boundaries," *Baseball Digest*, May 1999, 34–35.

58. Macnow, *Sports Great, Alex Rodriguez,* 49.

59. Bradley, *Alex Rodriguez,* 29.

60. Shalin, *Alex Rodriguez: A+ Shortstop,* 9.

61. Author's interview with Tom Grieve, March 8, 2006.

62. Author's interview with Brad Wilkerson, April 28, 2006.

Chapter 5

A LEGEND IN THE MAKING, 1999–2000

In 1999, the United States turned its attention to the impeachment of President Bill Clinton due to the Monica Lewinsky scandal.[1] In the meantime, the buzz surrounding Seattle revolved around the new ballpark that was being built for the Mariners' use. Soon they would vacate the Kingdome, a facility nearly every baseball purist described as cookie-cutter bland and sterile, for a beautiful park to be known as Safeco Field. Not only was it to be a state-of-the-art ballpark—as would be expected for a park with a price tag of nearly $400 million—but it also would have the charm that the Kingdome lacked.

Despite the budding excitement of the new facility, the start of the 1999 season was far from an auspicious one. Rodriguez's left knee began bothering him when, during the off-season, he was performing a drill that required him to leap over boxes. By the end of training camp, his condition had worsened significantly. Soon it became apparent that surgery was necessary for his torn cartilage, and the recovery process basically cost him the first six weeks of the season; he would play in just 129 games, the fewest of his career once he became established at the big-league level.[2]

Furthermore, there were early rumblings about where Ken Griffey Jr. and Rodriguez would be playing down the road. Griffey had a contract that would expire at the end of the season, and Rodriguez was eligible to become a free agent after the 2000 campaign. Rumors circulating the city had one or both of them being traded before their contracts ran out. Rodriguez deflected questions, saying that because it was a situation he had no control over, it was pointless to fret over it. He reassured his fans that he loved playing in the Mariners uniform.

At one point, Rodriguez said the team simply had to turn themselves into a championship-caliber team. If they would make moves to achieve that goal, "and get the pieces," he would be thrilled to stay in Seattle. If not, he wished to move to a contender, singling out the Rangers, Yankees, and Indians. By fall 1999, Griffey Jr. advised A-Rod, who felt as if he was living under "a microscope," not to rush his decision about where to play in the future. "Just go out and play," he said.[3]

In mid-May, with the Mariners a handful of games below the break-even point, Lou Piniella jotted Rodriguez's name in the lineup, and A-Rod responded with a homer against the Kansas City Royals in his first at bat. He was back with a bang. Keeping his power-and-speed motif going, he also stole a base, making good on his belated opening day. Soon Seattle clawed their way back to .500. However, matters soon skidded downhill. Rodriguez went into an abysmal slump, one that saw his batting average tumble from .315 to .287.[4]

This was a rare season in that Rodriguez did not make the All-Star Game because the American League manager, Joe Torre, had to either carry four shortstops on his squad or omit A-Rod, "whose injury in the first week of the season hurt his chance to make the mid-summer classic."[5]

Finally, on July 15, Safeco Field was ready. The cozy but sterilely unattractive Kingdome, a victim of implosion, had been hitter friendly, but Safeco's dimensions were deeper. Would this park, sluggers wondered, be a cool, aloof mistress; would it "play big" and deny them of some home runs? As recently as spring 2006, some experts ranked Safeco as the toughest hitters' ballpark in the majors.

One writer stated, "Privately, Rodriguez predicted that Safeco would 'be the worst hitting park in the history of the game.'"[6]

Perhaps, to some extent, he was being an alarmist. Through 2004, Rodriguez had hit .275 in Safeco, precisely 40 points lower than he had hit in the Kingdome, but his home-run ratios in the two parks were similar (34 home runs over 545 at bats in the older facility versus 60 homers in 1,087 trips to the Safeco plate).

In 1999, David Bell, who provided 20 home runs while playing second base, and Alex Rodriguez set an obscure record when they combined for 62 homers, most ever in the majors by middle infielders on the same team.

As a team, though, the Mariners faltered, dropping to a disappointing third place in the American League West at four games below .500 (79–83), a remote 16 games in arrears of Texas. Coming off two seasons in which a playoff berth seemed feasible but the cold reality was elimination from postseason play, Rodriguez was visibly upset. In 2002, he looked back upon this time period and called the 1998 and 1999 seasons two of his toughest years of his career.[7]

Rodriguez was not too pleased with his .285 batting average, the nadir of his career, but he did provide the Mariners with 42 home runs, 110 runs scored, and an additional 111 runs driven in. At the age of 24, an age when many players would be happy just to be breaking into a team's lineup, Rodriguez was already a five-time All-Star, a member of the 40–40 club, and was the third-youngest man to win a batting title.

A NEW MILLENNIUM

As gongs rang out to proclaim the first few seconds of a new millennium, it soon became apparent that computers were not about to crash, nor were airplanes doomed to plummet to earth. Conversely, 2000 was the year that "scientists [cracked the] human genetic code, providing nearly a complete set of biological instructions for human life."[8]

In the meantime, the Mariners did indeed decide to swap Griffey Jr. On February 10, 2000, they dealt him for Mike Cameron, Brett Tomko, and two other players. It was off to Cincinnati for the "Kid," where he would be reunited with his father, a coach on the Reds.

So, for the first time since the late 1980s, the Mariners spring-training camp opened without the presence of "Junior." The message from Seattle's front office seemed clear to Rodriguez—retool for the future and sacrifice the present—a message that did not sit well with their perfectionist shortstop.

Rodriguez was faced with several incendiary issues; rumblings were heard: Could the team, in fact, win without the slugging, personable Griffey Jr., and now that the Mariners were, in effect, *his* team, would he, just 25 years old, assume a more dynamic approach to becoming a true leader?

During spring training, perhaps in an attempt to assume the mantle of team leader, Rodriguez distributed T-shirts with the motivational slogan, "We're on a Mission to Win!" emblazoned across the chest. He assumed the corner locker, the honored spot of the team captain, and goaded his teammates to excel.[9]

Meanwhile, he also was badgered with the all-important question: Will you still be with the club come 2001? He placated the media and fans, commenting that he had dealt with far more adversity than this situation presented; he seemingly did not perceive the issue as a problem at all.[10]

By the 2000 season, *The Sports Encyclopedia: Baseball* stated, "A strength of the American League was its quality shortstops. Perhaps at no time in baseball history were so many exceptional shortstops gathered in one league. Entering the season, [Derek] Jeter, Rodriguez, and [Nomar] Garciaparra, the Rookie of the Year in 1997, the year after Jeter had won that award, were established as capable fielders with super bats. In 2000, Oakland's Miguel Tejada [who would go on to wrestle the 2002 MVP Award from A-Rod] joined that group."[11]

In this era of a glut of stellar shortstops, most experts felt Rodriguez had emerged from the pack as the alpha dog. Rodriguez once observed, "We all watch each other and try to outdo each other. I think we push each other to a higher level. Who knows? Maybe if you can be the best shortstop in the American League now, you can be the best player ever."[12] As if to add some oomph to that contention, he ran together a string of 50 errorless games from May 14 to July 7.[13] In an interview with *Sport* magazine, he analyzed his batting success, attributing it to "leverage. I'm tall, wiry. I have good mechanics, good wrists. I get my hands and the bat through the hitting zone real quick and lift the ball in the air." He noted that he had gone from seeing himself as a fine fielding shortstop but only a "15-home run guy" to a legitimate offensive threat. Mark Ribowsky called the A-Rod swing "buoyant" and seemingly "unhurried yet at the point of impact [his cut] turns the ball around with astonishing force."[14]

Although he was again selected to the American League All-Star unit, a knee injury prevented his appearance in Atlanta, host city of the 2000 classic.

According to author Kim Covert, Alex met with his wayward father in June and nervously greeted him with a hug; he had, she wrote, "learned to forgive him."[15]

The season wound down, with Seattle struggling to overtake Oakland for good or at least to edge out the Cleveland Indians for the wild card bid to postseason play. In the Mariners versus Angels game of September 30, Seattle needed a win in order to cling to their playoff hopes. Rodriguez, bogged down in a 3 for 29 slump, snapped out of it on a grand scale. He homered in the first inning, a two-run shot off Tim Belcher, chased home a teammate on a fourth-inning single, then, in the sixth frame, on his 40th homer of the year, collected three more runs batted in. He capped things off with a sacrifice fly in the final inning, good for a career-best seven-RBI evening. Final score: Seattle 21 and Anaheim 9.[16]

The Mariners had managed to ease their way into the playoffs once more. The division race had not been determined until the last day of the season. The Mariners came up a tad short, with a second-place finish, an agonizing half-game behind the Oakland A's, enough to irritate Tantalus himself. However, the pain was salved by the fact that the Mariners notched the wild-card berth.

Also, Rodriguez had to feel a sense of vindication. He observed, "It's a great feeling because people didn't think we could get here without Junior."[17]

Suddenly, the team was headed back to postseason play for the first time since 1997. They faced the Chicago White Sox in the American League Division Series. The Mariners pitching staff, which averaged 29 years of age, was unintimidated by Sox hitters such as Frank Thomas, holding him to three consecutive impotent days at the plate (zero for nine); overall, the White Sox hit .185 as a team. Like carpetbaggers of old, the Mariners swept into town (for two games in Chicago and the almost anticlimactic finale in Seattle), and then skipped town after figuratively pillaging the White Sox. Rodriguez contributed with his .308 batting average and a couple of runs batted in.

Next up: the defending world champion New York Yankees, with a trip to the World Series at stake. In the series opener, A-Rod drilled a sixth-inning payoff pitch, a fastball, from Denny Neagle. It hugged the line before sailing over the wall for his first American League Championship Series home run. That solo shot gave a one-run cushion to the 1–0 lead Freddie Garcia had clung to going into that inning and the bullpen held on, giving Seattle a 2–0 whitewash win.

Later, up two games to one, the Yankees sent ace Roger Clemens against Seattle. Writer Glenn Stout wrote, "The defining moment of the contest—and in fact of the entire postseason—came when Alex Rodriguez stepped to the plate with two out in the first inning." The Yanks had lost only five of their previous postseason games, with Clemens, inexplicably, being saddled with three of those defeats. "Two fastballs flew out of Clemens's hand toward A-Rod's head, and one of them sent him on his back.

"While Rodriguez reacted with a wry smile, Mariner manager Lou Piniella and the rest of the Seattle bench exploded."[18] Dugout detonation aside, Clemens had taken charge of the game with that 97 mile per hour fastball near A-Rod's jaw and then "threw his next pitch in almost the exact same spot." Mariners catcher Joe Oliver later commented that he felt "Clemens essentially beat the Mariners when he threw those two inside pitches to Rodriguez." From there he breezed to a 5–0 victory, fanning 15 and surrendering just one hit, an innocuous seventh-inning Al Martin line drive that ticked off Tino Martinez's mitt near first base.[19]

Although the Mariners did come back to take Game 5, the series would be extended to just one more contest. Orlando "El Duque" Hernandez topped them for the second time in the series to nail down the pennant for the Yankees. The October 17 defeat was to be Rodriguez's last game in the Mariners uniform. He had bowed out in fine fashion, his bat as sizzling as the sun of his parents' native land; he hit .409 against the Yankees with two homers and five RBIs.

All-in-all, the 2000 season had been quite a ride. Only shortstops Vern Stephens of the Red Sox (twice) and Hall of Famer Ernie Banks had ever played shortstop and driven in more teammates than Rodriguez's 132. Plus, he would go on to smash this personal high twice over the next two seasons. With Griffey Jr. gone, it certainly helped A-Rod's RBI quest when he moved into Griffey's old slot in the lineup.

Unable to reach an agreement with Rodriguez, the Mariners apparently were willing to lose him. On October 30, he was granted free-agency status. The Mariners, in losing Griffey and Rodriguez, had not merely whipped out a broom to clean house, they had taken an Oreck vacuum to the team, ending one era in Seattle.

Going into 2001, one publication called Rodriguez "the first player in the 25-year history of free agency to be established as one of the game's top few players and still have his peak seasons ahead of him at the time he entered the market." It was little wonder that he could command mind-boggling amounts of money. The publication also believed that his move to "The Ballpark in Arlington is going to bump Rodriguez's raw stats enough that he may finally get the MVP awards he's been denied so far." That prediction, especially as it called for multiple MVP trophies, was bold yet *almost* entirely correct.[20]

NOTES

1. Don Jensen, *The Timeline History of Baseball* (New York: Palgrave Macmillan, 2005), chart.

2. Mike Shalin, *Alex Rodriguez: A+ Shortstop* (Champaign, IL: Sports Publishing, 1999), 2–3.

3. Jim Gallagher, *Alex Rodriguez: Latinos in Baseball* (Childs, MD: Mitchell Lane, 2000), 58–59.

4. Ibid., 56.

5. John Lowe, "Aiming to Be the Best," *Baseball Digest*, October 1999, 47.

6. Tim Wendel, *The New Face of Baseball: The 100-Year Rise and Triumph of Latinos in America's Favorite Sport* (New York: HarperCollins, 2003), 201.

7. Michael Bradley, *Alex Rodriguez* (Tarrytown, NY: Benchmark Books, 2005), 32.

8. Jensen, *The Timeline History of Baseball*, chart.

9. Glen Macnow, *Sports Great, Alex Rodriguez* (Berkeley Heights, NJ: Enslow, 2002), 53.

10. Bradley, *Alex Rodriguez*, 33.

11. David S. Neft, Richard M. Cohen, and Michael L. Neft, *The Sports Encyclopedia: Baseball*, 23rd ed. (New York: St. Martin's Press, 2003), 666.

12. Macnow, *Sports Great, Alex Rodriguez*, 10.

13. Kim Covert, *Alex Rodriguez* (Mankato, MN: Capstone Press, 2002), 35.

14. Mark Ribowsky, *The Complete History of the Home Run* (New York: Kensington, 2003), 295.

15. Covert, *Alex Rodriguez*, 35–36.

16. Ibid., 36.

17. Macnow, *Sports Great, Alex Rodriguez*, 57.

18. Glen Stout, *Yankees Century: One Hundred Years of New York Yankees Baseball* (New York: Houghton Mifflin, 2002), 436.

19. Buster Olney, *The Last Night of the Yankee Dynasty* (New York: HarperCollins, 2004), 101.

20. Jeff Bower, Clay Davenport, Jeff Hildebrand, Gary Huckabay, Rany Jazayerli, Chris Kahrl, Keith Law, et al. *Baseball Prospectus: 2001* (Dulles, VA: Brassey's, 2001), 434.

The early years: Rodriguez takes a cut in Seattle. Photo: National Baseball Hall of Fame Library, Cooperstown, N.Y.

Rodriguez makes yet another fine defensive play. Photo: National Baseball Hall of Fame Library, Cooperstown, N.Y.

Rodriguez turns a double play for Seattle. Photo: National Baseball Hall of Fame Library, Cooperstown, N.Y.

Rodriguez's classic big cut. Photo: Brad Newton, DBA Newton Photography.

Autograph seekers cluster around the generous Alex Rodriguez. Photo: Brad Newton, DBA Newton Photography.

Rodriguez rips the ball as a member of the New York Yankees. Photo: John Grieshop/ Getty Images.

Chapter 6

THE LONE STAR YEARS, 2001–2003

The year immortalized in the title of sci-fi classic *2001: A Space Odyssey* was, on many levels, historic in the United States. This was, of course, the year of the terrorists' most devastating and craven attacks on the country, killing nearly 3,000 people on September 11. In the resilient world of baseball—where all games were canceled for a week (for "the first time that nonlabor-related events had shut down the game for that long since World War I"[1])—the surly Barry Bonds was about to embark on an unforgettable season in which he would jack the ball 73 times to shatter Mark McGwire's season record set just three years earlier. Sammy Sosa would top the 60-home-run plateau for the third time. Clearly, things were flourishing within the then blind-to-the-steroid-issue baseball community.

Although Latinos made up just more than 10 percent of the population in the United States, their impact on baseball was as forceful as the thunderous footfall of a T-rex. On opening day of 2001, almost 20 percent of major leaguers were Latino, "up from only 8 percent about fifteen years earlier." Over a five-year run from 1998 to 2002, almost one-third of all Gold Glove recipients were of Latin descent. It only made sense as baseball had been introduced to Latin America not long after it began widespread play in the United States; Cuba formed its first pro baseball league in 1868. The game spread like the process of osmosis throughout Latin America, to Mexico, Puerto Rico, and to the Dominican Republic.[2] As early as 1911, two Cubans, Rafael Almeida and Armando Marsans, were playing major-league baseball for the Cincinnati Reds.[3] Ozzie Smith felt that shortstops were the best athletes on the diamond and that Rodriguez, by this time, was "probably emerging not just as the best shortstop, but the finest all-around player in the game."[4]

Another slick shortstop, Mark Bordick, analyzed Rodriguez's glove work: "Alex is so deceptive out there. As much ground as he covers, as big as he is, sometimes it doesn't look like he's even moving, but he gets to balls deep in the hole and up the middle, and he has an incredibly strong arm."[5]

One of baseball's hottest topics was still Texas's signing of A-Rod back on December 11, 2000. Some experts felt that when he inked his astronomical $252 million, 10-year pact with Texas (it was actually a seven-year deal with player options for an additional three seasons), his aura of being baseball's golden boy dimmed. To some, he became the living symbol of what was wrong with the game of baseball; he was the personification of avarice. It was as if along with the slew of folding money he also accepted 30 pieces of silver. If, as he once said, money could not change him, it certainly could change the way others saw him, and controversy began to circle him like vultures in search of carrion.

Several issues quickly cropped up. First of all, Rodriguez obviously was under the glare of the media, as scalding as the Arlington, Texas, sun; was he worth the loot dished out or would he wilt?

Second, many fans perceived Rodriguez as a sort of modern-day mercenary. Yet few fans bothered to stop and think that if they, on their job, were suddenly offered a ton of money to transfer to another city or work for another company, they would jump. As pitcher Kevin Millwood observed, "I think there are probably people that dislike him because of his contract, but find one person that's going to turn that contract down. So I don't fault him at all for that and, you know what, the guy goes out and plays, and he plays hard. So be it. There's going to be people in this world who dislike you for stupid reasons, and I'm sure that's the same reason people dislike him."[6]

To Texas owner Tom Hicks, A-Rod was to be a savior, the one player to deliver the Rangers to the promised land of the World Series. Hicks originally had forked over $250 million to buy the Texas team just two years earlier, now he was signing *one man* to a contract worth $2 million more than that already celestially high figure.

Having bought then built the National Hockey League Dallas Stars into Stanley Cup champions, few doubted Hicks's intentions; he was hell-bent on paving the way for a Rangers world championship as well. He recently had finalized deals with some local cable television networks that "upped the value of his franchise. By signing the popular Rodriguez, he was able to ink additional marketing deals with companies."[7]

Hicks was adding A-Rod to a squad that already included such heavy hitters as Ivan Rodriguez, coming off a .347 season, and Rafael Palmeiro, destined for greatness (500+ home runs with more than 3,000 hits) and controversy (with charges of steroid use). The only question seemed to be did Hicks's team have enough pitching? Based on their finish on the bottom rung of the division the year earlier, and with the acquisition of Rodriguez seemingly indicating the team's ongoing emphasis on hitting over pitching, the answer seemed to be a resounding no.[8]

Some also felt the A-Rod situation was a bit baffling in that he repeatedly had spoken of his love for the city of Seattle and said his main concern was "Can we win? That's the only thing—a ring."[9] So, seemingly defying the logic of his own contention, he departed Seattle, where his Mariners had just made it to the playoffs, and headed to Texas, a team coming off a last-place finish.

Therefore, some mused that although Rodriguez had insisted he left the Mariners because he wanted to play for a contender, he actually was guilty of abandoning Seattle's ship, which had sailed to a fine 91–71 mark in 2000, in favor of the Rangers, with their mirror-image record of the Mariners, 71–91. True, Texas had won the American League West in 1998 and 1999, but they had won only one playoff game throughout their 40-year history. Perhaps, as one writer speculated, he set out to move to a club in which he would be the indisputable leader.[10]

Further, critics wondered if Rodriguez was simply rationalizing his departure from Seattle in favor of the big bucks of Texas. As it would turn out, Rodriguez's plans and hopes to help them become winners were doomed.

Ironically, the very year Seattle lost A-Rod, they became a juggernaut of a team and tied the single-season major-league record with 116 wins set by the 1906 Chicago Cubs (although the Mariners, who boasted a win-loss percentage of .716, did play 10 games more than the 1906 Cubs, who posted a blistering .763 win-loss percentage). Seattle, in notching two more wins than the mighty 1998 Yankees, created a new league record for victories in a season.

Despite dropping Rodriguez's contract from their books, the Mariners actually hiked their overall payroll in 2001, to $74 million, up $15 million from the year before.[11] Ichiro Suzuki was the new kid on the West Coast block, a sensation who wowed the league as a 27-year-old rookie—one with seven Japanese batting titles in his homeland—winning both the Rookie of the Year Award as well as the MVP and copping the batting crown.

Rodriguez had departed the Mariners "so he could play for a winner. In Texas, he experienced a rich contract, a great personal year, and a last-place team."[12] Indeed, Rodriguez's Rangers could muster only 73 wins. The humiliation was compounded when one took a look at the final standings and found Texas a flyspeck in Seattle's rearview mirror—a crushing 43 games behind the Mariners.

THE 2001 ODYSSEY

After a modicum of the tumult of Rodriguez's contract signing faded, the season had begun with Texas traveling to San Juan, Puerto Rico, for their opener versus the Toronto Blue Jays as major-league baseball continued its efforts to go global and create international goodwill. Texas proudly trotted Rodriguez out like a glistening, new trophy put on display.

Rodriguez booted his very first fielding chance with the Rangers, however; actually, he came up with the ball cleanly but his throw to first took off, sailing into the stands, for an error. On his next fielding opportunity, he slipped while trying to start a double play, and he later "fell on his face" attempting yet another play on a grounder. After banging out two hits, a single in his first Rangers at bat and a double, in an 8–1 defeat, Rodriguez took it all in stride, even the boos and sarcastic comments that he had heard. "You have to start somewhere. . . . You just move on."[13]

Moving on was not so easily accomplished at first, and after nine additional games, he remained sans home runs. Over the next series, a three-game set versus Oakland, he erupted with the force of a Texas stampede. He clobbered four homers and drove in 11 runs during the Rangers sweep and wound up taking American League Player of the Week honors.[14] Then, on April 16, Rodriguez was mugged, so to speak, by Seattle fans when A-Rod, as a new member of the Texas Rangers, made his homecoming to the Pacific Northwest. In 2006, Tom Grieve said he thinks, overall, A-Rod's image is still "very positive," but he acknowledged that many fans hold his huge contract against him. Grieve said, "I don't blame Alex for leaving Seattle, but the people in Seattle do. That was not a breakup that was amicable. I mean, many people *despise* him in Seattle, and in their mind they don't think he was genuine in the way he left. Most people look at Alex and say, 'He became a free agent, he was one of the most attractive free agents ever at a young age, he earned the contract because someone was willing to pay it to him, and most of us would have done the exact same thing.'" Still, as Grieve recalled, "I've never seen a more vitriolic crowd than that night in Seattle."

Ideally, Rodriguez would have liked to have been embraced the way Cal Ripken Jr. has been. "I would think that Alex, deep down inside, is a little bit envious of the fact that Cal, everywhere he went, was looked up to, admired, and cheered in every ballpark." Grieve agrees that A-Rod would "love to be appreciated the way Ripken was."[15]

The way one writer saw it, Seattle "fans were shocked that a goody-goody like Rodriguez could be mercenary to the extreme. A-Rod left tire marks in his haste to leave Seattle for the highest bidder."[16] As popular as he once was in a Mariners jersey, he was taunted unmercifully by bitter fans who felt Rodriguez had shed his Seattle uniform like a snake sheds its skin. Homemade posters mocked him, calling him "A-Wad" and "Pay Rod." One fan baited a fishing hook with money then dangled it toward him when he was in the on-deck circle, and others littered the field with bogus bills.[17]

After another game later in the year in Minnesota, fans cascaded cat-calls down on Rodriguez. He shook it off, observing, that, yes, "The volume has gone up a little bit on the Boo-O-Meter."[18] He realized he would have to develop an extra thick layer of epidermis to combat the criticism, and do so quickly.

Over a late-April and early-May stretch, things began to unravel rapidly, and Texas managed to drop 11 of 12 games, plunging them 14 games behind Seattle and into last place; things would only get worse. Rodriguez remained great, but had Texas placed too much stock in him? His salary represented 25 percent of the team's total $88 million payroll. By contrast, little money was allocated for pitchers; their five primary starters combined for $19.5 million, less than A-Rod alone. By far, the bulk of the payroll went to him, Rafael Palmeiro, and Ivan Rodriguez.[19]

On May 12, Rodriguez made history when he connected against the White Sox in the second inning for career home run number 200. Only four men had reached that milestone at a younger age. He added another homer in the ninth, good for his sixth run driven in, but his personal pyrotechnic display was not enough. In a contest that could well have served as a microcosm of the entire season for A-Rod and the Rangers, the Chicago White Sox prevailed in a 12–11 slugfest.

The 2001 All-Star Game rolled around, and Rodriguez's childhood hero, Cal Ripken Jr., was to start the contest at third base, his spot since moving there from shortstop, where he had roamed for 15 years, in 1997. In the meantime, A-Rod again led fan voting and was the starting short-stop that night. Moments after the two took their positions on the left side of the infield, however, Rodriguez gestured to Ripken to switch spots with him. Only when the Orioles legend saw Joe Torre, the American League manager, motioning from the dugout to make the move did

Ripken reluctantly slide over to his old stomping/fielding grounds. So Ripken, in his final big-league season, not only started the game, but he also made a token appearance at shortstop.

Mastermind Rodriguez had set the whole thing up ahead of time, devising the plot and suggesting it to Torre shortly before game time; Torre immediately approved of the tribute.

Tom Grieve recalled, "I think what Alex was saying was, 'You may have switched to third base, but everybody, when they think of Cal Ripken, thinks of shortstop, and I may be playing shortstop right now, but you're the player that I most admire, and the only thing I can think to do to honor you right now is to defer to you and let you move over to shortstop, where you will get the right to go out of this All-Star Game in your last [one], playing a position that everybody remembers you at.' I think he did it out of admiration and respect."[20]

Although that was a nice, sentimental gesture, Ripken's home run and his subsequent MVP honors were sheer baseball drama. Rodriguez had helped make Ripken's final All-Star appearance a very special one.

On the regular season, due to shoddy pitching and defense, the Rangers plunged into last place, losing 89 times. Not even Rodriguez's punch was enough to bolster the team's plight.

His contract had nine years left to run, and Texas's return for their money in 2001 was fine: .318 batting average, a stunning 52 homers, and an impressive 135 RBIs.

At the start of the season, Rodriguez had been asked if the contract carried with it an addendum that gave him a degree of pressure that matched the impact of the money. He replied saying that, money aside, every trip to the plate is packed with pressure and that he intended to deal with such pressure as he always had, with "desire and determination." He said he had never been hungrier than he was the day he signed the contract and that he was motivated by baseball, not cash. He was correct; he shrugged off any extraneous pressure and, as always, excelled.[21]

His 52 home runs now stood as the most ever by a big-league shortstop, well beyond Ernie Banks's 47 homers from 1958. His slugging percentage was worthy of an emphatic, "Wow," at .622. The archaic concept of shortstops being punchless officially was pronounced dead.

Even his RBI total placed fourth as the most potent shortstop output ever, and, more awesome, he accumulated 393 total bases, also the most ever by a shortstop in a season. On defense, only two shortstops had more than his 751 total chances. Plus, despite playing on a loser, A-Rod finished sixth in the MVP voting, once again finishing one slot behind Juan Gonzalez.

The 2001 season also put Rodriguez a bit closer to his Hispanic heritage. Because there were so many Spanish-speaking players on the Rangers, he felt compelled to "brush up on his Spanish." At times with teammates, he said he would actually forget to speak in English. He also noted that for Latinos baseball was rather "like a cult" or a religion.[22]

2002: RODRIGUEZ'S YEAR OF CLOUT

For the 2002 campaign, Rangers owner Tom Hicks vowed to boost his team's fate by adding arms. His thought process was correct, but his acquisitions, such as Todd Van Poppel, Chan Ho Park, and Ismael Valdes, were not.

This year, Rodriguez celebrated his 27th birthday by crushing one home run early in the game and topped that off with a game-winning grand slam in the 10th. He would later comment that he hoped people eventually would take a retrospective look at his consistently brilliant career and not be able to distinguish "when my free-agent year was." He further gushed how he loved the game of baseball and how that was what kept him going, even during seasons when his team slogged through disappointment.[23]

On August 17, 2002, Rodriguez smashed three homers. One day later, he wrote his name into baseball's record book yet again. He became just the sixth man in big-league history to compile five straight 40-plus home-run seasons. He was in illustrious company with sluggers such as Babe Ruth, Ralph Kiner, Sammy Sosa, Ken Griffey Jr., and Duke Snider.

Nine days later, Rodriguez hit an unusual home run off Orlando Hernandez in that it came off the seldom-seen "eephus" (or blooper) pitch, the same pitch served up by Rip Sewell to Ted Williams for a famous All-Star Game homer.

As the season was winding down, heading into September, Rodriguez, who had played many a game with a bad ankle, was on a roll, hot as an erupting radiator. He was driving home runs with such regularity he was averaging almost one RBI per game, concluding the season at a scorching-hot 142 RBIs. Rodriguez wound up with 57 home runs, giving him two legs up on the Triple Crown while nearly joining Babe Ruth, Roger Maris, Mark McGwire, and Sammy Sosa as the only men ever to pile up 60 homers in a season.

He also became just the third player ever to hit 50 or more homers while displaying the smooth defense it took to win a Gold Glove, his first; he made just 10 fielding misplays in 741 chances, a career high. The only others ever to accomplish a 50 home run season coupled with a Gold Glove were the graceful Willie Mays in 1965 and former teammate

Griffey Jr. in 1998. Also, no shortstop ever hit as many homers in a season as A-Rod, who had upped his personal best of the previous season by five; and the National League best by Ernie Banks remained a remote 47. Only seven men ever had hit more than Rodriguez's 57 home runs, all huge names such as Babe Ruth and Hank Greenberg.

He also now owned back-to-back seasons with 50 or more homers. The only other men to manage that were Mark McGwire, Sammy Sosa, Babe Ruth, and Ken Griffey Jr. As one publication put it, "Alex Rodriguez hit for the kind of numbers that put left fielders in the Hall of Fame."[24] He also displayed durability, riding to season's end on a 386-consecutive-games-played streak; hardly Ripken-like, but noteworthy, nevertheless.

Although Texas lost 90 ball games and again finished in the dank cellar of the American League West, A-Rod's numbers gleamed so brightly that there was support for him winning the league's MVP trophy. Historically, the likelihood of this happening was a nearly impossible; after all, only four MVPs ever had come from a team with a record below .500, and only Andre Dawson labored for a last-place club. Regardless, said Rodriguez with confidence and without a trace of pompousness, "I deserve it." With history and the odds on Miguel Tejada's side, however, it was no shock when division-winning Oakland's fine shortstop hauled home the MVP hardware. He easily outdistanced Rodriguez 356 votes to 254, largely on the strength of his 21 first-place votes versus a mere 5 for A-Rod.[25]

Toronto's general manager, J. P. Ricciardi, said that although he felt Rodriguez was the best player in the league and might wind up someday as the best baseball player of all time, Tejada, by definition of the word *valuable*, deserved the honor. Furthermore, Hal McRae, who was managing the Tampa Bay Devil Rays, said succinctly, "You can't be that valuable when you're on a last place club." Those words would soon prove to be untrue.[26]

To cap off his magnificent year, Rodriguez took longtime girlfriend Cynthia Scurtis for his bride on November 2, not long after the baseball season had wound down. Scurtis was a psychology teacher at a Florida high school, described as a woman of "strong faith."[27] By the way, one source stated that Rodriguez has "a long-term desire to teach" as well. He stated that after his baseball career comes to an end, he wants to become a civics teacher and a basketball coach.[28]

THE LAST OF THE LONE STAR YEARS

By 2003, "195 of 750 players on major league rosters on Opening Day speak Spanish as their first language." In world news, a coalition led by the United States attacked then occupied Iraq, removing Saddam Hussein from power.[29]

Going into the season, the Rangers acquired additional pitching to bolster their woeful staff from 2002. Believing a closer could help their cause enormously, Texas obtained Ugueth Urbina, a hard-throwing pitcher, to serve as their closer.

In the springtime, many baseball purists barked their displeasure when they learned of the collective salary of the New York Yankees. They both rued and resented the $185 million payroll, and their protests reverberated that the mighty Yanks were out to "buy" the pennant—which they seemingly did, only to fall to the upstart Florida Marlins in six World Series contests.[30]

In the meantime, back on April 2, Rodriguez again etched his name in the record books when he became the youngest player ever to belt 300 home runs, usurping the former record holder, the prodigious Jimmie Foxx, by 79 days. Rodriguez was a mere babe at 27 years and 249 days old, but a babe with near-Ruthian power.

The month of May was miserable for the Rangers, and team owner Tom Hicks finally conceded that it was time to cast off some of his marquee players and allow prospects the chance to mature at the big-league level. Whether this was the right course to take, it was clear to Rodriguez that his goal of a world championship under this regime was, at least for the foreseeable future, unattainable; in his mind it was a deja vu scenario harkening to when his Mariners had jettisoned Randy Johnson and Ken Griffey Jr.

As the season wore on, Rodriguez, though still productive, was unable to carry the load himself; Texas floundered through a 7–20 June, and things would not get much better all year long. They wound up 20 games beneath .500 at 71–91, a mortifying 25 games behind the Oakland A's, about as ineffective as a faith healer's blow to a supplicant's forehead.

There was no lack of success on A-Rod's part, though, as he starched the ball with nova intensity. He swatted 47 home runs to lead the league in that category for the third successive season. He drove in 118 runners while leading the league in runs scored at 124 and while hitting a solid .298. Not only that, but his error total of eight marked the lowest of his career, and he led all American League shortstops in double plays while also ranking among the best for assists and putouts. He earned another Gold Glove Award; like the message of an old television commercial, he was not getting older, he was getting better.

The end of the 2003 season marked the end of Rodriguez's days as a Ranger (and, for all intents, as a shortstop). It was the end of the line for an astoundingly productive era there: He averaged an amazing 52 homers per year for Texas. He played in every game, save one, of a possible 496 games, despite what baseball experts labeled an unforgiving Texas sun that, some say, is a major factor in the Rangers lack of significant success over the years.

For the third consecutive season, he captured the Hank Aaron Award as the top hitter in the American League. The former record for the most seasons with 100 or more runs driven in by a shortstop was five, held by Joe Cronin. In 2003, A-Rod topped 100 RBIs for the sixth time (and it is a pretty safe assumption that he would have kept the streak alive had he continued to play shortstop with the Yankees).

With yet another big home-run season behind him, Rodriguez had put a record once held by another Cubs player, Ernie Banks, deep into baseball's archives. Shortstop A-Rod now owned six consecutive 40-plus home-run seasons—tied with Sammy Sosa (1998–2003) for the second-longest skein ever, trailing only Babe Ruth's seven in a row—to just four for Banks. In fact, "only a handful of players have ever had six seasons of 40-plus homers, much less consecutively." Also, all of them save Rodriguez played first base or the outfield, the traditional power positions.[31]

In November, when the balloting for the MVP Award was released, Rodriguez had pulled off a rarity: He had won the trophy while languishing with a last-place team.

Tom Grieve said, "It's hard for me to vote for a player on a last-place team to be the Most Valuable Player, it just doesn't compute. You can come out with the 'best player' statistically, but how valuable could you be to a last-place team. But, what happened in [Andre] Dawson's year and what happened in Alex's year was on the good teams, the contenders, there was no clear-cut choice to be MVP. And then I think the voters said, 'Well, look, because there's no one on the Red Sox, Yankees, A's, whoever, deserving of a real MVP vote, now's the time to recognize a player who's had more than an MVP season.' And that's why Alex won it."[32]

Rodriguez felt he should have won the honor the previous season with the cellar-dwelling Rangers, but now came a degree of reaffirmation of his greatness. He informed the media that he felt "humbled and overwhelmed."[33]

Rodriguez also informed the press that despite his no-trade clause in his contract with the Rangers, he was all in favor of a trade to a contender. Circumstances were ripe for mammoth machinations in the near future.

Perhaps Tom Grieve captured it best, "I got to watch A-Rod for three years here in Texas. We got a unique look at him, and I don't think there's any doubt that he is one of the greatest players in the history of baseball, and when he's done playing, he *may be* the best player in the history of baseball. He came here with a huge contract, which was a huge burden for him to bear, and no player could possibly have played better for the Rangers for [the] three years that Alex did. He was perfectly prepared, in great shape, he played everyday, he worked as hard as anybody on the team, and he put up numbers offensively and defensively that were off the charts.

"Baseball, however, is a sport that's not the same as basketball where you sign Shaquille O'Neal and go from [being] a last-place team to a championship team—doesn't work that way in baseball. I think that [the] signing of Alex is probably the best example of that. Tom Hicks paid him a lot of money, and Alex gave him everything that you could possibly buy in a player, but it didn't do much for the team because one player can't impact a team that way. But he was a joy to watch, he was fun to be around, he was always talking baseball on the plane and in the clubhouse, and he played hard every single game."[34]

What more, Rodriguez might wonder, could one want out of him?

NOTES

1. David Nemec and Saul Wisnia, *100 Years of Baseball* (Lincolnwood, IL: Publications International, 2002), 508.

2. From Bob Costas's introduction in Tim Wendel, *The New Face of Baseball: The 100-Year Rise and Triumph of Latinos in America's Favorite Sport* (New York: HarperCollins, 2003), xi–xii.

3. Ibid., 7.

4. Paul Post, "Ozzie Smith Rates Alex Rodriguez Best All-Around Player in Majors," *Baseball Digest*, May 2001, 37.

5. Larry Stone, "Shortstop Star Power," *Baseball Digest*, May 2001, 35.

6. Author's interview with Kevin Millwood, April 28, 2006.

7. Elliott Kalb, *Who's Better, Who's Best in Baseball?* (New York: McGraw-Hill, 2005), 74.

8. Glenn Stout, *On the Field With . . . Alex Rodriguez* (New York: Little, Brown, 2002), 115.

9. Wendel, *The New Face of Baseball*, 201.

10. Ibid., 202.

11. Kalb, *Who's Better, Who's Best in Baseball?* 73.

12. David S. Neft, Richard M. Cohen, and Michael L. Neft, *The Sports Encyclopedia: Baseball*, 23rd ed. (New York: St. Martin's Press, 2003), 678.

13. Michael Bradley, *Alex Rodriguez* (Tarrytown, NY: Benchmark Books, 2005), 37.

14. Ken Rappoport, *Super Sports Star Alex Rodriguez* (Berkeley Heights, NJ: Enslow, 2004), 40.

15. Author's interview with Tom Grieve, March 8, 2006.

16. Mark Ribowsky, *The Complete History of the Home Run* (New York: Kensington, 2003), 314.

17. Hogan Chen and Adam Green, "Alex Rodriguez," *BaseballLibrary.com: The Home*

of Baseball History (2006), Available at http://www.baseballlibrary.com/ballplayers/playe.
php?name=Alex_Rodriguez_1975.

18. Rappoport, *Super Sports Star,* 7.

19. Kalb, *Who's Better, Who's Best in Baseball?* 74.

20. Author's interview with Tom Grieve, March 8, 2006.

21. Glen Macnow, *Sports Great, Alex Rodriguez* (Berkeley Heights, NJ: Enslow, 2002),
59.

22. Wendel, *The New Face of Baseball,* 202.

23. Ibid., 199.

24. Neft, Cohen, and Neft, *The Sports Encyclopedia: Baseball,* 23rd ed., 690.

25. Bradley, *Alex Rodriguez,* 39, 40.

26. Ibid., 40.

27. Marylou Morano Kjelle, *Alex Rodriguez: Professional Baseball Player* (Hockessin, DE:
Mitchell Lane, 2006), 25.

28. Steve Riach, *Heart of a Champion: Profiles in Character,* with John Humphrey (Nashville, TN: Broadman and Holman, 2001), 17.

29. Don Jensen, "Timeline Introduction," *The Timeline History of Baseball* (New York:
Palgrave Macmillan, 2005), chart.

30. David S. Neft, Richard M. Cohen, and Michael L. Neft, *The Sports Encyclopedia:
Baseball,* 25th ed. (New York: St. Martin's Griffin, 2005), 702.

31. Kalb, *Who's Better, Who's Best in Baseball?* 75.

32. Author's interview with Tom Grieve, March 8, 2006.

33. Stout, *On the Field With . . . Alex Rodriguez,* 123.

34. Author's interview with Tom Grieve, March 8, 2006.

Chapter 7

THE BIG APPLE
ERA BEGINS, 2004

The 2004 season was destined to be the most lucrative one in baseball history, with the 30 big-league teams luring a record 72,968,953 fans through their turnstiles. Spectators of Rodriguez's first major-league team, the Mariners, were treated to Ichiro Suzuki's hitting barrage as he wound up breaking George Sisler's record for hits in a season (257) when he lashed out for 262 safeties. Elsewhere, Randy Johnson continued to dominate, firing a perfect game for the Diamondbacks.[1]

Sadly for Rodriguez and the Texas Rangers, their dream of building a perennial contender with him never materialized. As a matter of fact, Texas finished in the cellar three years running, with meager win totals of 73, 72, and 71. Instead of progressing, the actually had skidded backward.

Not long after that gloomy 2003 season ended, Rangers owner Tom Hicks approached Boston, asking them if they would swap their shortstop Nomar Garciaparra, a two-time batting champ, and some of their young pitchers to Texas in exchange for Rodriguez. Hicks felt he had to jettison A-Rod's hefty salary. Mindful of the old baseball line, "We can finish last without you," Hicks simply felt that paying a fortune for one player only to *still* finish in last place could not be tolerated.[2] It was clear that A-Rod had peeled off his Texas Rangers garb like so much detritus for the final time.

The Red Sox gained Commissioner Bud Selig's permission to negotiate with Rodriguez, and by early December the Red Sox's intentions had leaked to the media. It soon became apparent that Garciaparra almost certainly would not re-sign with Boston. Another twist occurred when the Red Sox countered the proposed trade of super shortstops by saying they would be willing to part with slugger Manny Ramirez in exchange for A-Rod. Had that deal been consummated, it would have featured a trade involving baseball's two largest contracts ever, a swap involving the only players earning $20 million or more.[3]

By December 17, the transaction appeared to be a done deal, needing only the approval of Selig and the Major League Baseball Players Association. Players Association Deputy Director Gene Orza lobbed an oversized monkey wrench into the works, however, when he pointed out that some of the details of the trade violated the basic agreement between union and management: Boston had asked Rodriguez "to restructure his contract to ease the immediate fiscal burden" on them, offering Rodriguez deferred payment. In the eyes of the Players Association, A-Rod, by agreeing to accept a restructured contract, was, in effect, buying "his way up the American League food chain" from Texas to Boston.[4] Even though Rodriguez would gain from the deal—he "would be guaranteed additional marketing rights and would be allowed to become a free agent after the 2005 season"—the union did not want to set a precedent by "decreasing the value of the largest player contract" ever, so they fought the restructuring.[5]

At that point, the Red Sox "wouldn't budge," refusing to listen to a counteroffer, and one of the most monumental trades in the annals of baseball "was dead."[6] Reportedly, the Red Sox lost Rodriguez over a matter of $12 million, hardly chump change,[7] but considering Rodriguez's stature and track record, it was an amount that would not deter the Yankees from pursuing the perennial All-Star.

So, though Boston technically had acquired Rodriguez for a matter of a scant few hours, the Yankees persevered and obtained him in what ESPN's baseball expert Tim Kurkjian basically labeled the largest trade in baseball's history.[8]

Boston had felt so utterly defeated when, in the waning moments of 2003, in the 11th inning of Game 7 of the American League Championship Series, Aaron Boone snatched elusive, tantalizing success from them. So, they "rededicated themselves to winning the World Series a year later." Despite such zeal, they lost Rodriguez in the "front office's ferocious off-season war with the Yankees." That once again helped fuel the teams' feud, as would the fact that the two venerable teams, possessing the two highest payrolls in the game, had met a gut-wrenching 26 times over the 2003 season, more than any other two teams ever over the course of a season.[9]

The Yanks eventually wound up with Rodriguez because, in mid-January 2004, Aaron Boone, of all people, ruptured his anterior cruciate ligament during a pickup basketball game. He would miss the entire 2004 season, forcing the Yankees to seek a new third baseman. Ultimately, that man, of course, was Rodriguez.[10]

On Valentine's Day, a Long Island newspaper announced Rodriguez would wear a Yankees uniform in 2004 and that the Rangers had acquired standout second baseman Alfonso Soriano and a player to be named later, which turned out to be infielder Joaquin Arias. The Rangers did consent to pay a bundle of cash, about $67 million of the remaining $179 million on Rodriguez's contract. Thus, the Yankees had replaced their number eight hitter in the batting order, Boone, who was earning about $5 million, while taking on an additional $112 million. They believed Rodriguez was well worth the investment, even though they now had four men earning "in excess of $100 million" and the left side of their infield was to take home "more in annual salary than the entire Milwaukee Brewers' roster. The projected Opening Day line-up for the Yankees would earn about $85,000 *per inning.*"[11]

The press also revealed that Rodriguez was quite willing to become the Yankees' new third sacker. The Yankees had pulled off a coup, doing in secret talks over a four-day span what Boston had fumbled away over a period of a couple of months. What further allowed Yankees fans the right to gloat was the fact that the Red Sox walked away from consummating the blockbuster of a deal due to an insignificant (by Boston and New York standards) sum of money. New York newspapers ran headlines such as "Summer or Winter, the Yankees Show the Red Sox How to Win." The following month, Yankees owner George Steinbrenner, responding to criticism by the Sox front office, fumed, saying that Boston, "unlike the Yankees" failed "to go the extra distance" in trying to get A-Rod and please their fans. Like a stern father, Selig had to step in between the quarreling siblings, ordering all such insults to cease. The intensity of the Boston-New York feud was dog-days-of-August hot, and the season had yet to open.[12]

A-ROD'S INTRODUCTION TO NEW YORK

At the February 17 press conference that introduced the newest Yankee to the media, Rodriguez observed that the decision to sign with the Yankees was not a difficult decision at all. He said that it all "came down to winning."[13] As for the specific Boston versus New York issue, A-Rod was placatory in his comments; for example, he stated he had been close to signing with the Sox several times, but that he was now happy to be a Yankee.[14]

Also at the press conference, Reggie Jackson, a former Yankee, commented, "This could have been happening in Boston, but somebody fell down." He continued by ripping the Red Sox for valuing money over the acquisition of a superstar and summed up the situation, "Twelve million is huge for normal people but not the people running baseball, especially when it comes to arguably the best player in the game."[15]

Jackson also agreed with Rodriguez's assessment that it all boiled down to winning. He stressed the Yankees' philosophy that winning a division title was not fulfilling enough for them. "It's not about winning 112 or 114 regular-season games around here," he began, "it's about winning eleven games in the postseason [the requisite amount to win the world championship]."[16]

Boston felt they could never quite match the Yankees, could not get over that annoying highway rumble strip, so to speak. Over the past six seasons, dating back to 1998, the standings in the American League East had remained unchanged. Each year, the Yankees had finished first over the Red Sox, followed by Toronto, Baltimore, and Tampa—every single year. In 2004, the Yankees had to plug in new pitchers to replace stars Roger Clemens, Andy Pettitte, and David Wells, but they were still preseason favorites to once again relegate the Red Sox to a second-place finish. This season marked the 102nd year of head-to-head play involving the Sox and Yanks; entering the year, New York held the advantage 1,047 wins to 854.

During Rodriguez's first trip to New York, no longer a Ranger or Mariner, he was greeted by a huge banner that adorned Yankee Stadium, "A-Rod, Welcome to New York."[17]

Rodriguez was joining a team with a glorious history, a franchise that dates back to 1903, which had won 8,996 regular-season games, and which had laid claim to 26 world championships and 39 pennants, by far the best in baseball. On the other hand, his two former teams were among the only three American League teams never to have won the championship (Tampa Bay being the other team of futility). A-Rod was joining the franchise of Mickey Mantle and Joe DiMaggio and Lou Gehrig and Babe Ruth.

As a side note, because Ruth's number 3 jersey number had long been retired, A-Rod, who had also worn that number in Seattle and Texas—in fact, he had worn number 3 since he was 10 years old—would have to switch. He settled on number 13, the number his all-time favorite quarterback, Dan Marino, had worn with the Miami Dolphins (and which Rodriguez also wore as a high school quarterback).

Despite the Yankees' legacy, they did have their work cut out for them. For instance, they never had finished in first place for six consecutive seasons, and that was their first goal en route to a world championship ring.

Of course, critics ripped Yankees owner George Steinbrenner, leveling charges that the A-Rod acquisition was tantamount to once again trying to "buy" the pennant. Many saw Steinbrenner as an owner who possesses the ardor of a baseball card collector, bent on acquiring every star he can get his hands on, from Reggie Jackson to Randy Johnson. He was likened to a bully determined to play, but only on an uneven playing field, using the financial clout of his Yankee empire rather than fists and ominous words. On February 17, he addressed those allegations, denying he went out and bought Rodriguez, arguing that Texas obtained a fine player in Alfonso Soriano. He barked that the media should "look at the finances before you make that statement." Still, a look at Steinbrenner's recent off-season moves seems to validate the "buying the pennant" cries: He obtained pitcher Mike Mussina before the 2001 season, slugger Jason Giambi prior to the 2002 season, star outfielder Hideki Matsui for 2003, and A-Rod along with yet another slugger, Gary Sheffield—and reloaded further by adding high-priced pitchers Kevin Brown and Javier Vazquez (having lost Roger Clemens, David Wells, and Andy Pettitte)—to open the 2004 campaign. The contracts of the five hitters exceeded $520 million. As writer Mike Vaccaro wrote, "Only the Yankees could foot that bill."[18]

A-ROD JOINS JETER

At any rate, Rodriguez was thrilled to finally become a teammate with longtime friend Derek Jeter. They had first met when they were quite young, a few months after initially talking over the phone, having been introduced by a common friend. Jeter was in Florida for the start of his second season in pro ball and offered advice to Rodriguez, still in high school, about his dilemma of going pro versus attending the University of Miami.[19]

Both winners of the Gatorade Award, which—according to the New York Yankees media guide—is given to the national baseball student athlete of the year they immediately related to each other. Rodriguez later would write that they had so much in common, "it's like looking in the mirror" and that when their teams had squared off against each other in the past, the players would room not in their respective team's hotel but at each other's house. Also, Rodriguez noted that they were able to "talk out our unique frustrations with each other." Jeter, who, in 1992, was the first high school player taken in that year's draft, once commented that he loved Rodriguez "like a brother. . . . We both work hard. We both understand we're blessed by the opportunities we have, and we try to be good people."[20]

Later, their discussions often centered on defense, not hitting, because, as Rodriguez said, "That's what a shortstop's game should be about." He said they both felt they would rather suffer through an "oh-fer" (hitless game) and help out with their leather than enjoy a perfect day at the plate and lose. He added, "Nothing justifies an error."[21]

When Rodriguez was still with the Mariners, Jeter had commented that he was Rodriguez's "biggest fan. I brag on him so much that my teammates are sick of me talking about him." He related how after A-Rod would hit a homer versus the Yankees, "he'll go sit on the bench and flex his arms at me."[22]

Although the mutual admiration society image may seem a bit Pollyanna-like, and although some jaded New Yorkers anticipated a clash of egos between the two shortstops, no such occurrence took place at first. As a matter of fact, by mid-April, one writer noted that the two men were virtually inseparable and, due to a strong facial resemblance, "could have been mistaken for brothers." All was well on the Yankees left side of the infield.[23]

In the eyes of some baseball fans, the question of who *should* hold down the shortstop position came up—of who was the better shortstop, Rodriguez or Jeter. In spring training, some Yankee fans got on Jeter for not making the move to third base for Rodriguez, but in the eyes of A-Rod, coming off his second Gold Glove season in a row, it was a nonissue. He would make the move to third, magnanimously so, and Jeter would continue to cover the hole between second base and third. Some found it telling that Rodriguez had not told Boston that if they traded for him, he would be willing to play third so their sensational shortstop, Garciaparra, could continue to play at that defensive spot.[24]

Tom Grieve was reluctant to compare Rodriguez to Derek Jeter because of the respect he has for both players. "In fact, Jeter is one of my favorite players. I love the way Jeter plays the game and everything about him. I like the way he represents the Yankees and the respect for the game that he has, but strictly from a scouting standpoint, some scouts may feel that Alex is physically a more talented shortstop.

"But Alex knew going in that if he wanted to be a Yankee it would have to be as a third baseman. Jeter was the shortstop, an All-Star, Gold

Glover, and a .300 hitter with four World Series rings who was the leader of the Yankees.

"They will both go into the Hall of Fame. Alex might go in being recognized as the better player, but Derek will go in recognized as one of the greatest of all Yankees, one of their greatest leaders with his own plaque in monument park. It could go down as the best left side of any infield in the history of baseball."

In his 2006 preseason interview, Grieve continued, "The other thing about Alex is he proved that he was defensively one of the top shortstops in the game; he won a Gold Glove at shortstop. So, he didn't have to prove that to anybody; everybody already knows that. Now he can take pride in the fact that he's moved to a new position and he's a Gold Glove caliber player at that position."[25]

Rodriguez's former double-play partner at Texas, Michael Young, said of A-Rod's early transition to third base, "He's done a fine job. The tough part about is now you're starting [to be compared to] a bunch of guys who have played third base their whole lives; those guys have set the bar pretty high. Alex is such a good shortstop it's still kind of hard to visualize him at third, but he's doing a great job over there."[26]

For the record, baseball experts agree that A-Rod is a better shortstop than Jeter. Writer Steven Goldman called Jeter a player who was "seriously overvalued by fans and management alike" and went on to assert that "by every defensive metric known to man, Jeter's defense had been dismal—perhaps even untenable—for years. From 1999 to 2003, Jeter had posted five of the most damaging defensive seasons by a modern shortstop (post-1901) in the history of the game." Over that span, he averaged giving up almost 19 runs a year more than the average big-league shortstop. Further, Goldman mentioned that there had been only one shortstop other than Jeter who was allowed to keep his job at shortstop after posting even *three* such poor defensive seasons. Normally, a shortstop who is so lacking does not even retain his job after one such year. Goldman also contended that moving Jeter to third, or even to second base or center field, where the Yankees most needed to plug in a player, made much more sense, but the Yankees chose to keep Jeter at short to assuage his ego.[27]

Young noted, "Derek had been playing shortstop in New York for close to eight, nine years at the time, so no one's going to tell Derek he's not doing his job anymore regardless of who's coming in. Alex, at the time, was winning Gold Gloves and putting up great numbers, so he was probably the best shortstop in the game, but if you're going to go to the Yankees, you're not going to play short, so that was his call, his decision, and the Yankees obviously liked it."[28]

In any case, it was patently clear that Jeter and A-Rod formed a great duo. As Yankees General Manager Brian Cashman said, "We have argu-ably the best left side of the infield in baseball history." Rodriguez, for example, had hit 40-plus homers over each of his last six years and owned seven 100-RBI seasons. Now he was determined, he said, to win not just one or two championships, "but hopefully help create a legacy as one of the [best] Yankee teams of all time."[29]

A-ROD'S YANKEE TENURE BEGINS

True to his almost monomaniacal work ethic, Rodriguez reported sev-eral days early to spring training to work out with former Yankees great third baseman Graig Nettles. He spoke of how delighted he was to be with a winner. "I was eliminated from contention in early May or late April the last couple of years," he said. "I've had enough of last place." He obliquely stated that his goal was to make it to the World Series, too, saying that he was looking forward to playing at Yankee Stadium in "over ninety games."[30]

Inevitably, the venom-laced blood that existed between the Red Sox and Yankees would be spilled. Rodriguez, who observed of the two teams, "If you didn't like watching New York-Boston last year, there's something wrong with you," was soon to be in the 2004 mix of things.[31]

The first exhibition meeting between Boston and New York took place on March 7 in Florida at Boston's camp at Fort Myers's City of Palms Park, exactly 143 days since Game 7 of the 2003 American League Champion-ship Series. Reportedly, more than 250 members of the media covered the encounter, "about ten times" the norm for a Boston spring training game, and, on eBay, a seller was asking $500 for two tickets to the stand-ing-room-only contest.[32] In *Emperors and Idiots*, author Mike Vaccaro has tickets selling for as high as $1,000 on eBay that morning.[33] "Journalists beat the drums of overhype." It was ludicrous; after all the hoopla, Erick Almonte wound up playing more at third base than Rodriguez in a truly meaningless contest.[34]

It was transparent that already A-Rod was playing in a circus atmo-sphere for a team former Yankees Cy Young Award–winning pitcher Sparky Lyle had nicknamed the "Bronx Zoo." In any event, early during the regular season, the Red Sox hosted the sluggish Yankees, with New York "struggling, still legless," coming directly off an arduous journey, to open the regular season.[35] They just had taken a flight from the United States to Japan, where they played Tampa Bay at 5:00 A.M. EST, and after two games with the Devil Rays and two exhibition contests, they were whisked back to Florida for more spring training games. Seven games later, they wearily trekked to Boston for a four-game set over Patriots' Day weekend.

Jeter stated, "We try to say it's [the rivalry] not different, but it is. It just is." He was quite correct; the opening game of the set marked the 15th straight time the two clubs met when they stood first and second in the American League East, going all the way back to April 2001. That, researchers unearthed, was the longest such skein in major-league history.[36]

When the dust from the diamond cleared at the end of the weekend, Rodriguez, his bat as effective and as potent as a soggy loaf of French bread, had gone an anemic 1 for 17 over three Yankees defeats to the delight of the four-game throng of 140,000 Fenway fans. In fact, his first 16 trips to the plate resulted in zero hits and six strikeouts—this from a hitter who hardly *ever* suffered through three straight hitless games; only twice before had he taken an 0 for 12 in a series.[37]

Joe Torre laughed it off a bit, saying that perhaps Rodriguez, who had always worn jersey number 3 but switched to 13 due to the unavailability of 3 (retired by the Yankees in honor of Babe Ruth), should change to yet another number, dumping the "unlucky" 13.[38]

Yankees General Manager Brian Cashman did not fret at all. "You can't keep a good player down," he insisted. He felt Rodriguez would acclimate himself to the glare and the fanfare of all that is New York, just as men such as Roger Clemens, Patrick Ewing, and Mike Piazza had to do. He continued, "I think big names in the big markets, you have to walk through the fire first. It's human nature to put a lot of pressure on yourself and try to perform at a higher level." He felt positive that by the end of the year Rodriguez's stats would be fine.[39]

The New York media did not help matters. When Boston made their first trip into town on April 23, sweeping a three-game set and giving them six wins over seven meetings, one newspaper doctored a photo of A-Rod sitting in the dugout so that the bench seemed to be ablaze. The headline read, "A-Rod on Heat Seat."[40] The Yanks were hitting .217; A-Rod, despite his first Yankee Stadium homer as a Yankee on April 24, was just over .250, and even Jeter was being booed at home. Their losing record represented the latest date that the team was under .500 since April 22, 1997.

On May 4, A-Rod hit his 350th homer, making him, at 28, the youngest man to accomplish this. He also drove in four to surpass the 1,000 RBI plateau. Only Mel Ott and Jimmie Foxx ever managed that feat at a younger age.

When Rodriguez returned to Texas for a late-May three-game set, fans there gave him the same treatment Seattle fans had given him when he first traveled to that city in a foreign uniform. Tumultuous boos reverberated during each of his at bats.

Then, during the nationally televised New York at Boston game of July 24, the slow-burning wick of their feud finally reached the powder keg. A brawl was imminent, and A-Rod, thrust into and caught up in the two teams' cauldron, was right in the middle of it.

The night before, A-Rod led New York with a ninth-inning hit off the wall. That hit, coming with first base open, chased home the game-winning run and upped the Yanks lead in the division to nine-and-a-half games. Naturally, the Yankees hoped the Sox would continue to slumber, but they were, on this fateful, soggy, somniferous day, about to, as the baseball cliché goes, "awaken a sleeping giant."

With two outs in the third inning, the Yankees, nursing a 3–0 lead, sent Rodriguez to the plate to face Bronson Arroyo, a pitcher he had gone up against in high school. A-Rod was feeling good about his situation, coming off his dramatic hit off the Green Monster one day earlier. He said that clutch hit was his "first official big hit to make me a Yankee."[41]

Then it happened. Arroyo's first pitch bore inside, striking Rodriguez close to his left elbow. Rodriguez reacted, taking a step toward the mound and then barking out his displeasure, figuring he just had been plunked as payback. As Boston catcher Jason Varitek, who intervened on Arroyo's behalf, recalled, "He started yelling at my pitcher." Presently, Varitek tested Rodriguez's tensile strength, experimenting to see how long it would be until he snapped. Varitek insisted there was no intention on Arroyo's part to drill the Yankee star and stated, "I told him to get to first base. He yelled back at me, said the F-word a couple of times and 'Come on,' and eventually it came on." It, of course, being the donnybrook. An unsubstantiated rumor later had Varitek baiting Rodriguez with a snide, "We don't bother hitting .260 hitters."[42]

What Varitek did for sure, however, was shove his catcher's mitt into A-Rod's face, and he followed that up with a wrestling move, hoisting Rodriguez off the ground. Bench-clearing fisticuffs ensued, with Rodriguez at the center of the maelstrom. Yankee starting pitcher Tanyon Sturtze skirmished with Gabe Kapler, grabbing him around his neck before being swarmed by David Ortiz and Trot Nixon. Sturtze emerged from the scrum, bloodied and with a slight finger injury. The bad blood that already had existed between these two clubs was now infected.

When order was restored, the fight's two principles, along with New York's Kenny Lofton and Kapler, were all ejected from the game. In the bottom half of the inning, Boston rallied against Sturtze, taking a 4–3 lead. The game, like the brawl itself, was a wild one. Although the Red

Sox were down, 10–8, in the last of the ninth, a Kevin Millar RBI single drove in Garciaparra, who had led off the frame with a double, and Bill Mueller's two-run, walk-off homer against the normally infallible Mariano Rivera (with a string of 23 consecutive converted saves under his belt) ended the nearly four-hour-long Boston marathon, giving the Sox a highly satisfying 11–10 victory. Over their previous 56 games, the Yankees had not dropped a single decision when holding the lead entering the ninth.[43]

Later, Rodriguez was asked if his first glance at the intensity of the rivalry gave him an insight into its virulence and ugliness. He grinned, "Put it this way, it isn't love."[44] In retrospect, the fracas was called a turning point and the event that galvanized the Red Sox, helping them, albeit a few weeks after the brouhaha, to turn their seemingly moribund season around. David Ortiz commented that the altercation was "the best thing that ever happened to us," even though the truth is Boston did not springboard their way to success immediately after the incident. The Sox did not actually spurt until August 7, when they began a 19–4 win-loss binge.[45]

At any rate, when Rodriguez finally finished serving his four-day suspension, he returned to the lineup on August 19 and promptly homered.

Ultimately, on September 30, the Yankees once again secured the division title and became only the fourth team ever to win more than 100 contests three straight years. The Red Sox then captured the wild-card berth, having finished second behind the Yankees for the seventh consecutive season. Rodriguez prophesied, "I think the road to the World Series is somehow going to go through New York or Boston." He was, of course, correct.[46]

THE REGULAR SEASON'S AFTERMATH

Down by a game in the second battle versus the Minnesota Twins in the American League Division Series, the Yankees entered the bottom of the 12th trailing by a run. However, Rodriguez, who wound up the series hitting .421, came up with a key double, and the Yankees prevailed. Likewise, in the conclusive Game 4, they had to overcome a four-run deficit as late as the eighth inning, again winning in extra innings. Once more, A-Rod came up big, banging out an 11th-inning double, swiping third base, and then scoring the winning run, scampering home on a wild pitch. Next up: the Boston Red Sox.

Going into the 2004 American League Championship Series (ALCS), Reggie Jackson spoke about how he felt Rodriguez was so talented and how he might end up being considered a great postseason player. Still, he said that in order for that to happen, Rodriguez would have to step it up a notch when all the eyes of the baseball community were boring in on him. "Some guys," began Jackson, "don't have the makeup for it. You can't be a Yankee if you don't have the makeup. You have to have a certain makeup to perform and excel here."[47]

The Yankees opened at home and quickly displayed the right stuff in Game 1, capturing a 10–7 slugfest. Game 2 was a tight one, a 2–1 Yankees win. In front of a shell-shocked Fenway Park crowd, Boston lost again, this time in a mortifying 19–8 debacle. A-Rod hit .429 through the first three frays.

On the brink of extinction, the Red Sox battled back, taking a 6–4 decision in a heart-palpitating 12 innings. Buoyed, Boston also won Game 5, this time in a grueling 14-inning bout.

The Red Sox continued to cling to their baseball life, winning the next controversy-filled contest 4–2 in front of a hostile New York throng, forcing the necessity for a Game 7.

Incidentally, what once may have been said somewhat in jest, but now appeared prophetic, years earlier Rodriguez had stated that winning was so all-important to him, he would "even cheat to win." In light of the karate chop he executed on Bronson Arroyo in Game 6 of the ALCS (discussed in chapter 2), his quote and his actions tarnished his image.[48]

It did not help matters when, in the series finale, Rodriguez hit harmless ground balls and whiffed, prompting boos from the frustrated home crowd. The Yankees' bats, normally loud, booming, and productive, had gone silent while Boston exploded. In the second inning, Johnny Damon's grand slam made it 6–0, Boston; it was, as fans say, time to stick a fork in the Yankees, they were done.

The eventual 10–3 defeat marked the first time in baseball history that a team down three games to zero stormed back to win a seven-game postseason series; the loss was devastating. Mariano Rivera blew saves on consecutive nights, and the top four Yankee hitters—Jeter, Rodriguez (who went 2 for 17 in Yankee losses, including a paltry 1 for his last 15 at bats, and was 0 for 7 with men on base), Sheffield, and Hideki Matsui—combined to hit nearly .500 in the first three games, then took a nosedive, hitting .167 over the last four games. One publication accused A-Rod of disappearing "in the clutch."[49]

A dejected Rodriguez, his bat having gone silent, said he was embarrassed and that he was through with baseball until the following spring; he would not even watch the World Series on television.[50]

He lingered at the park until 3:00 A.M. and would later comment that he would never forgive himself or the Yankees for this loss because he found it unfeasible that they could have lost four consecutive contests "to anyone."[51]

Yankee general manager Brian Cashman likened Boston to the *Halloween* character Jason. "We thought we had them down and out, but they came back and hunted us."[52] The Red Sox were fated to win it all, whereas A-Rod and the Yankees, glum and stunned, were headed home.

Rodriguez did, however, find some solace that off-season when, in November, Cynthia and he had their first child, a daughter they named Natasha.[53]

Rodriguez also could take some comfort from what he had achieved in his initial year with the Yankees. Sure, his .286 batting average was his lowest since 1999, but he did produce a plethora of runs, scoring 112 times and driving in 106; that marked the eighth year in a row he crossed home plate 100 or more times and his seventh consecutive season with 100 or more RBIs. He also fell just two steals shy of the 30-30 level for homers and stolen bases.

One publication stated that he "started putting up numbers only after he was moved to second and protected by Sheffield in the line-up."[54] At any rate, by most accounts it was a very solid, but not spectacular, season, even though he helped the Yanks win 101 times and generated enough votes to finish 14th in MVP balloting.

Some people had wondered how the dimensions of Yankee Stadium would impact Rodriguez. Aside from the fact that, as the baseball cliché goes, "he can hit 'em out of any park including Yellowstone," he did wind up hitting more home runs on the road (19) in 2004 than he did at home (17). As a visiting player in Yankee Stadium, however, he had managed 14 lifetime homers over 173 at bats, good for one home run per every 12.36 at bats, compared to his lifetime (through 2006) rate of a homer for every 14.58 at bats. Plus, over his first three years as a Yankee, he would hit .314 at home versus .285 on the road.

Rodriguez and Gary Sheffield gave the Yankees their second ever duo of right-handed hitters with 30-plus homers; the first time that happened was way back in 1940. Additionally, the Yanks had six players with 20 or more homers for just the second time in team history (joining the 1961 edition of the Yankees: Mantle, Maris, et al.).

In 2005, Elliott Kalb's *Who's Better, Who's Best in Baseball?* was released. The book ranked baseball's greatest 75 players ever. Rodriguez was listed as the ninth best of all time, trailing only luminaries such as Babe Ruth,

Willie Mays, Hank Aaron, and Ted Williams. Kalb was impressed with what A-Rod had accomplished in just nine full seasons. For instance, only 10 players owned a better lifetime slugging percentage: 5 of them outfielders, 4 of them first basemen, and only Rogers Hornsby, like Rodriguez, an infielder. Kalb also felt the single most vital stat in baseball is runs scored, in that the main goal of the game is to cross home plate. He noted that over Rodriguez's nine-year stretch (1996–2004), he averaged 122 runs each season, best in the bigs.

Kalb cited Rodriguez's adeptness at getting himself into scoring position through stolen bases and his truckload of extra-base hits, 701 over the nine-year span. Again, that put him number one among his contemporaries, ahead of Barry Bonds, Sammy Sosa, and Jeff Bagwell, and his 376 homers trailed only Sosa (442) and Bonds (411) for total homers from 1996 to 2004. "In the greatest nine-year stretch of Barry Bonds's career, he out-homered A-Rod by just 35 home runs (less than four per season)."[55] Metronome steady, A-Rod had, based on a full 162-game year, posted a seasonal average of .307, 44 home runs, and 125 RBIs through 2005. Such numbers are the stuff of legends.

NOTES

1. David S. Neft, Richard M. Cohen, and Michael L. Neft, *The Sports Encyclopedia: Baseball*, 25th ed. (New York: St. Martin's Griffin, 2005), 714.

2. Dan Shaughnessy, *Reversing the Curse: Inside the 2004 Boston Red Sox* (New York: Houghton Mifflin, 2005), 41–44.

3. Mike Vaccaro, *Emperors and Idiots: The Hundred-Year Rivalry between the Yankees and Red Sox—From the Very Beginning to the End of the Curse* (New York: Doubleday, 2005), 11.

4. Ibid., 12.

5. Steven Goldman, ed., *Mind Game: How the Boston Red Sox Got Smart, Won a World Series, and Created a New Blueprint for Winning* (New York: Workman, 2005), 35.

6. Shaughnessy, *Reversing the Curse*, 41–44.

7. Another source says Selig had given "the Red Sox and Rodriguez 72 hours to again restructure the contract. Boston asked that he slash his contract by $28 to $30 million, which he union blocked." Elliott Kalb, *Who's Better, Who's Best in Baseball?* (New York: McGraw-Hill, 2005), 76.

8. Shaughnessy, *Reversing the Curse*, 46.

9. Ibid., 10, 13.

10. Ibid., 44.

11. Buster Olney, *The Last Night of the Yankee Dynasty* (New York: HarperCollins, 2004), 323.

12. Shaughnessy, *Reversing the Curse*, 46–48.

13. Michael Bradley, *Alex Rodriguez* (Tarrytown, NY: Benchmark Books, 2005), 41.

14. Shaughnessy, *Reversing the Curse*, 49.

15. Vaccaro, *Emperors and Idiots*, 186.

16. Ibid.

17. Marylou Morano Kjelle, *Alex Rodriguez: Professional Baseball Player* (Hockessin, DE: Mitchell Lane, 2006), 7.

18. Vaccaro, *Emperors and Idiots*, 188, 229.

19. Stew Thornley, *Alex Rodriguez: Slugging Shortstop* (Minneapolis, MN: Lerner, 1998), 23.

20. Alex Rodriguez and Greg Brown, *Hit a Grand Slam* (Dallas: Taylor, 1998), 36.

21. Jim Gallagher, *Alex Rodriguez: Latinos in Baseball* (Childs, MD: Mitchell Lane, 2000), 42.

22. Mark Stewart, *Alex Rodriguez: Gunning for Greatness* (Brookfield, CT: Millbrook Press, 1999), 36, 39.

23. Shaughnessy, *Reversing the Curse*, 91.

24. Vaccaro, *Emperors and Idiots*, 172.

25. Author's interview with Tom Grieve, March 8, 2006.

26. Author's interview with Michael Young, April 28, 2006.

27. Goldman, *Mind Game*, 52–53.

28. Author's interview with Michael Young, April 28, 2006.

29. John Kuenster, "A-Rod and Jeter May Become Best Duo Ever on Left Side of Infield," *Baseball Digest*, June 2004, 17, 20.

30. Vaccaro, *Emperors and Idiots*, 187.

31. Shaughnessy, *Reversing the Curse*, 50.

32. Ibid., 65.

33. Vaccaro, *Emperors and Idiots*, 11.

34. Goldman, *Mind Game*, 47.

35. Shaughnessy, *Reversing the Curse*, 87.

36. Ibid., 88.

37. Goldman, *Mind Game*, 80.

38. Shaughnessy, *Reversing the Curse*, 88.

39. Ibid., 95, 96.

40. Ibid., 96.

41. Ibid., 144.

42. Ibid.

43. Ibid., 146.

44. Vaccaro, *Emperors and Idiots*, 205.

45. Goldman, *Mind Game*, 171–172.

46. Shaughnessy, *Reversing the Curse*, 172.

47. Vaccaro, *Emperors and Idiots*, 318.

48. Mike Shalin, *Alex Rodriguez: A+ Shortstop* (Champaign, IL: Sports Publishing, 1999), 73.

49. Bob Nightengale, "House of Ruth Shaken to Foundation," *USA Today Sports Weekly*, October 27–November 2, 2004, 11–12.

50. Shaughnessy, *Reversing the Curse*, 210.

51. Ibid., 211.

52. Nightengale, "House of Ruth Shaken to Foundation," 12.

53. Kjelle, *Alex Rodriguez: Professional Baseball Player*, 25.

54. Nightengale, "House of Ruth Shaken to Foundation," 12.

55. Kalb, *Who's Better, Who's Best in Baseball?* 72.

Chapter 8

ANOTHER YEAR, ANOTHER MVP, 2005

As 2005 began, Rodriguez glanced back a year and called 2004 "by far the toughest year of my career. It was a very challenging year and I'm better for it." He also conceded that "New York's a handful, and I just felt I tried to please too much. I'm more comfortable now."[1]

By now, Rodriguez's stats and accomplishments devoured eight pages of the *New York Yankees Information and Record Guide*. In March 2005, Joe Torre was asked if the stinging 2004 defeat to Boston would spur the 2005 Yankees' determination. He replied, "Well, I'm happy to say that we've been there [the World Series] more times than anybody else over the last nine years. So, sure, it was disappointing last year, but in order to reach it as many times as we've reached it, there's nothing that motivates us more than our own ambitions. Obviously, with the Red Sox, our number one rival, snatching it away from us last year, you can't wait to get back on the field again, but you can't have anything that you say motivates you more than what you're already motivated by. I don't know how much harder you could play."

He conceded only that losing to their rivals "intensified all the attention, there's no question. I'm sure if you asked a lot of people, the only thing they do know is the Red Sox beat the Yankees. They're not sure who they played in the World Series, but that's fine, that's what the rivalry is all about. The fact that we had a 3–0 lead [in games] and a lead in the ninth inning [of Game 4] made it very frustrating for us. At no time did we think that we had it in our back pocket."

Torre added that he was curious, now that the issue of the Boston dry spell of championships dating back to 1918 was out of the way, how things would play out "because the Curse is not the motivating factor, I'm not sure if the rivalry is going to be the same because that was part of how the fans used to haunt each other." He need not have worried; the acrimony between fans of the two cities endured, and by the end of the year the two clubs would have met 90 times over the last four years, splitting the wins in the endless encounters.[2]

On opening day, less than three weeks after players such as Sammy Sosa, Jose Canseco, Mark McGwire, and Rafael Palmeiro appeared and testified at a congressional hearing on steroids, Major League Baseball's first announcement revealing that a player was suspended for violating the new policy concerning performance-enhancing drugs was made. The controversy continued to crash on the baseball scene like violent ocean waves battering a small coastal town as Tampa Bay's Alex Sanchez, who denied using steroids, was suspended for 10 days.

In the meantime, one writer observed Rodriguez's batting average had dipped each season from his .318 in 2001 to .286 in 2004, the second-lowest average he ever had hit over a full season in the big leagues.

Amid such negativity, five-time Cy Young Award winner Randy Johnson, acquired from the Arizona Diamondbacks in yet another George Steinbrenner coup, made his Yankees debut. Johnson, known as the "Big Unit," clicked, topping Boston, and, for the moment, all was right in the kingdom of the New York Yankees. That was soon to change.

After being swept by the Baltimore Orioles over the weekend of April 15–17, dropping their record to 4–8, Steinbrenner was apoplectic. "Enough is enough," he proclaimed. "It is unbelievable to me that the highest-paid team in baseball would start the season in such a deep funk. They are not playing like true Yankees."[3]

On April 26, Rodriguez cracked three homers and added a run-scoring single, making him one of only a dozen men ever to drive in 10 or more runs in a game. Each home run—a three-run poke, followed by a two-run shot and a fourth-inning grand slam—came with two outs. He hit all three off Bartolo Colon, against whom A-Rod boasted a lifetime batting average of .425. Only four men ever had more than his 10 RBIs, with 12 being the best ever. In fact, Rodriguez came up just one run driven in shy of the American League record. He also became one of a few men to hit three homers in a single contest with three different clubs.

Despite such an onslaught, overall things had not gone well since Johnson's win to open the year back on April 3, and May 6 found the Yankees continuing to flounder; they stood at 11–19, the first time they had been eight games under .500 since way back on June 21, 1995. The most recent disheartening loss came when they dropped a game to Oakland, with the

A's scoring three times in the 10th inning without hitting a ball out of the infield. That saddled the usually infallible Mariano Rivera with the loss. In addition, they had lost 8 of their last 10 contests and shared the cellar with the hapless Tampa Bay Devil Rays.

On May 15, Yankees skipper Joe Torre won his 1,800th game, ranking him 13th all-time, and Randy Johnson registered career win number 250, but, emblematic of the somehow out-of-sync Yankees, he uncharacteristically failed to fan a batter for the first time in almost five years. And on June 1 the litany of Yankees troubles continued when Johnson was knocked off by the lowly Kansas City Royals for the first time since May 1993, breaking an unblemished 9–0 slate against them. This was the same Royals team that would finish the year a bleak 50 games below .500.

Right around this time, Rodriguez announced publicly for the first time that he was attending therapy sessions. His motivation to make such a revelation was, according to USA Today Sports Weekly, "in hopes that it might lift any stigma that kids feel about asking for help in their personal life."[4] His wife, who holds a degree in psychology, stated, "It's because of therapeutic intervention that he's been able to . . . flourish as a person." Alex added that baseball had almost nothing to do with his sessions.[5]

Shortly after copping the American League Player of the Month Award for May, A-Rod mused about his long-term future, beyond the end of the 10-year contract he had signed through 2010. "I haven't made my mind up yet on anything. I don't know what I'm going to do. I'd be lying if I said I'd play at 40. I'd be lying if I said I'd play at 35. It's still five years away."[6]

In any event, on June 8 the introspective Rodriguez placed another stamp on his place in history, annihilating a pitch, driving it for his 400th career homer. That made him the youngest of the 40 men to reach that milestone, surpassing the record held by Ken Griffey Jr. Rodriguez required 29 years, 316 days to reach his 400th; Griffey needed 30 years, 140 days. Furthermore, only A-Rod, Griffey, and Jimmie Foxx owned 400 or more homers before attaining their 31st birthdays. Then, with a win on July 18, the Yankees hoped their struggles were over as they finally emerged in first place, just ahead of Boston. At one point in June, the team with a $204 million payroll—baseball's first payroll greater than $200 million—had resided in last place, with only 10 big-league clubs playing more poorly. One writer had called the 2005 Yanks "the worst team money can buy." With a former All-Star at every position in the lineup, good for 53 total All-Star appearances, however, the team was bound to be resilient.[7]

Rodriguez celebrated his 30th birthday on July 27 with the knowledge that he was ahead of the pace of numerous all-time record holders. When Hank Aaron, all-time home-run and RBI king, was 30, he owned

342 homers and had driven in 1,121 runs; A-Rod had accumulated 409 homers and 1,176 RBIs. At the age of 30, Pete Rose had chalked up 1,540 hits; Rodriguez had 1,825. He was also ahead of the early paces of Rickey Henderson for career runs scored and Tris Speaker for lifetime doubles.

The season continued to be one of baseball's most turbulent ever as Palmeiro made headlines again, this time for his 10-day suspension for using steroids. Back in March, an indignant Palmeiro emphatically told a congressional panel, "I have never used steroids. Period." Now he was insisting he had ingested them, but accidentally. The 40-year-old slugger became the seventh, and by far the most famous, player to fail a test under the toughened big-league policy that began in March.

In what now may seem like a case of foreshadowing, on August 21, the White Sox, who would go on to win the 2005 World Series, tattooed Johnson for six runs and four homers over a period of just 16 pitches during a disastrous fourth inning.

SEASON'S END: MIXED REVIEWS

By season's end, Rodriguez had hit a lusty .321 (number two in his league) while driving in 130 runs and, once again showing his versatility, threw in 21 stolen bases. Perhaps most impressive, he lead the league, for the fourth time in five years, in homers (48). That feat etched his name in the all-time Yankees record book as it allowed him to surpass Joe DiMaggio's hallowed 68-year-old team record for the most home runs by a right-handed hitter. A-Rod became the first player ever to rap out more than 40 homers with three different clubs. He also won his first Silver Slugger Award as a third baseman.

An injury to Derek Jeter forced A-Rod to return to shortstop three times in 2005. He flawlessly handled each assignment. Through 2005, Rodriguez remained one home run shy of Cal Ripken Jr.'s all-time record for homers by a shortstop: 345.

The Yankees and Red Sox battled down to the wire, to their last series of the season—the first time since 1949 that the Yanks ended the year with a series that would determine a title. Tickets were going for as high as four figures. Boston won the opening game but dropped the second game when Rodriguez crushed a homer off a Tim Wakefield knuckler in Fenway and added three more hits. When the dust had blown away like so much infield dirt after a hard slide, Boston and New York were tied in the standings, both posting a lustrous 95–67 record. The Yankees finished a bit shy of becoming the first team ever to win 100-plus contests over four consecutive years. It was New York, though, that won the division, their eighth straight title, based on the head-to-head play tiebreaker. The Red Sox had to settle for the wild-card path to the playoffs.

New York boasted a $64 million pitching staff, but like the comedic jalopy straight out of a Disney cartoon, it putt-putted and spurted its way through the season at times, riddled by injuries, aches, and pains. In short, "At times, the Yankees also looked old."[8]

While the Red Sox were bowing out in five games against the juggernaut Chicago White Sox, New York took on the team with baseball's bulkiest, clumsiest name: the Los Angeles Angels of Anaheim. In the set, Rodriguez went a dismal 2 for 15 (.133) with no runs driven in and lamented that he had "played like a dog." The Angels thwarted the Yanks in Game 5 even though ace starter Bartolo Colon left the contest with a stiff shoulder sustained while facing the leadoff batter of the second inning. From there on, 22-year-old rookie Ervin Santana took over, breezing until late when Francisco Rodriguez—known as "K-Rod"—took over.

Rodriguez would say later that he wished he would have been somewhat more patient at the plate against the Angels during the frustrating American League Division Series. The Angels pitchers worked him very cautiously, and Rodriguez, who had hit .390 versus their staff during the regular season, helped them by going after pitches rather than taking some of them. During the regular season, he had fanned 139 times, third worst in the league. He felt his mistake "at the end" was in being a bit overanxious. "My one regret is I thought I could have walked 10 or 12 times and really just passed the baton and been a little bit more patient."[9]

Writers began speculating as to just when the decapitation of Joe Torre and/or general manager Brian Cashman would occur; how long would it take until Steinbrenner's ax fell, they wondered. It hardly seemed fair; Torre had been compelled to employ 14 starting pitchers, the most he ever used on his watch as the Yankees manager, and age and injuries had also hurt.

Although Torre's troops had lost to the Angels, over his first 10 years with the Yankees he had averaged a sweltering hot 98 wins per season, good for a .608 win-loss percentage. Further, in postseason play Torre's troops owned a stellar 73–38 record (.658), including 21 victories and the second-highest World Series win-loss percentage among men who had been there three or more times.

By way of comparison, venerable managers Tony La Russa and Bobby Cox have posted mediocre numbers in the postseason. Through 2005, La Russa's win-loss record was a mere one game over .500 (28–27), and Cox stands at exactly .500 (66–66). Winning in the playoffs is no easy task.[10]

Significantly, when the season had opened, there were 204 players on big-league rosters who were born in Latin American countries. That represented nearly 25 percent of baseball's major-league talent. Leading the way was the Dominican Republic with 91 players, followed by Venezuela with a distant 46 and Puerto Rico with 34.[11]

Earlier in the year, Chevrolet announced it would present the Major League Baseball Latino Legends Team based on fan balloting. Prior to the start of Game 4 of the World Series, that team was announced. It included Rodriguez at shortstop and fellow players of Dominican descent: Albert Pujols at first base, outfielders Vladimir Guerrero and Manny Ramirez, and pitchers Pedro Martinez and Juan Marichal. Fittingly, the talent-rich Dominican Republic dominated the 12-man squad.

Commissioner Bud Selig commented, "Over the years, Major League Baseball has been blessed with a wealth of players of Latin American heritage who have contributed to some of the most memorable moments and accomplished some of the most storied feats in the history of the game." Naturally, A-Rod felt great pride at being included in such a glowing commendation.[12]

As a matter of fact, the year he had signed his megamillions contract with the Rangers, realizing he was the highest-profile Latin player in the country and perhaps the world, he commented, with a strong sense of self-realization, "I know what I mean to all Latinos."[13]

The next honor Rodriguez was up for was the American League MVP Award. Now, nearly every single professional athlete involved in a team sport is highly competitive, and although some may protest that they do not really care about individual awards, they are, by and large, lying. Human nature is such that people want, even crave, recognition for their achievements. An old joke illuminates this condition: What do you call a player without a modicum of ego? Answer: an amateur. Baseball's greats, as a rule, have, at the very least, a healthy sense of ego. Given Rodriguez's drive and desire to excel, he had to covet the 2005 Most Valuable Player Award trophy.

Furthermore, given that, he had to have spent some fitful minutes waiting for the official announcement. Experts predicted a photo finish in the MVP race, much like the American League East Division race between the Yanks and their Red Sox rivals (in which, for the *eighth* year running, New York finished first with Boston in second place). After all, even Rodriguez openly admitted Boston's designated hitter David Ortiz was a huge force in the American League. Ortiz had carried Boston on his broad shoulders, hitting 47 home runs, hitting .300, and driving in a major-league-leading 148 RBIs. All of that helped guide the Sox into the playoffs.

Rodriguez conceded, "He is the one special player right now, like Barry Bonds, who can change the game around simply with his batting." His quote could be construed as a slight dig against Ortiz, who, unlike the Yankees third baseman, rarely plays the field. Sure enough, the Associated Press led off their story of Rodriguez's winning the MVP by stating, "Alex Rodriguez showed slick fielding counts . . . defeating David Ortiz in a vote that rewarded an all-around player over a designated hitter."[14]

A-Rod also was quoted as saying, "I think defense, for the most part, being a balanced player and also saving a lot of runs on the defensive side, I think was a major factor here. To me, defense is foremost. It's always been."[15]

The final voting was fairly tight, with Rodriguez receiving 16 first-place votes and 331 points overall to Ortiz's 11 first-place votes and 307 total points from the Baseball Writers' Association of America. An oddity: Only Barry Bonds and A-Rod ever had won two MVP Awards while wearing a different jersey number. When Rodriguez won his first MVP, his childhood idol, Keith Hernandez, presented the trophy to him; this time, Ripken Jr. was on hand to do the honors.

Aside from the painful failure to advance in postseason play, it had been another rewarding year for the 30-year-old Rodriguez. He had led the league in runs scored (124). In addition, he reached base a league-best 301 times, a personal high; led the league in slugging; and was second in on-base percentage with his career-high .421. Still, he had yet to exorcize the personal demons, the ones that taunted him, reminding him he had yet to win a World Series.

NOTES

1. Bob Nightengale, "Yankees Dynasty Hanging by a Thread," *USA Today Sports Weekly*, June 15–21, 2005, 6.

2. From Joe Torre's press conference, Bradenton, Florida, March 4, 2005.

3. Seth Livingstone, "Yankees Getting Cranky, Creaky," *USA Today Sports Weekly*, April 20–26, 2005, 29.

4. *USA Today Sports Weekly*, June 1–7, 2005, 15.

5. Cecil Harris, *Call the Yankees My Daddy* (Guilford, CT: Lyons Press, 2006), 228.

6. *USA Today Sports Weekly*, June 8–14, 2005, 14.

7. Nightengale, "Yankees Dynasty Hanging by a Thread," 4.

8. Seth Livingstone, "Questions Surround AL East Powers," *USA Today Sports Weekly*, October 12–18, 2005, 46.

9. Associated Press.

10. Associated Press.

11. Associated Press, "Players In Majors Born Outside U.S. Jumps" *Puerto Rico Herald* (April 7, 2005), available at http://www.puertorico-herald.org/issues2/2005/vol09n14/Media1-en.html.

12. "Major League Baseball and Chevrolet Unveil Program Celebrating the Greatest Latino Players in the History of the Game," *General Motors Corporate Website* (August 23, 2005), available at http://www.gm.com/company/gmability/community/news/chevy_mlb_082305.html.

13. Glenn Stout, *On the Field With . . . Alex Rodriguez* (New York: Little, Brown, 2002), 114–15.

14. Associated Press.

15. Associated Press.

Chapter 9

THE YEAR OF BOOBIRDS, OF FRUSTRATION, OF DISCONTENT, 2006

Events leading up to the start of the exhibition schedule were, in typical Yankees fashion, turbulent. Foremost may well have been the Ozzie Guillen affair in February, a big to-do concerning who Rodriguez should play for in the inaugural World Baseball Classic (WBC). First, though, some background: As far back as 1999, a quote appeared in a book on Rodriguez quoting him as saying, "I want to be known as Dominican—that's what I am, 100 percent. . . . I have a duty and responsibility to continue the legacy of Dominicans in baseball."[1]

Rodriguez was accused of vacillating (he denied that charge) before finally opting to play for Team USA. The fiery, outspoken Guillen, born in Venezuela, lashed out at Rodriguez in a February 20, 2006, *Sports Illustrated* piece by S. L. Price, unleashing his seemingly off-the-cuff thoughts in a rapid stream-of-consciousness style. He believed A-Rod had never seriously considered playing for the Dominican team and labeled him a hypocrite. Soon after his comments went public, he backpedaled, apologizing to Rodriguez. Joe Torre spoke to the Associated Press concerning the issue, which had simmered for a few days but which had been left unstirred by Rodriguez, "There's a lot of jealousy out there. That's what goes with who you are, how much you make and all that stuff. It's part of the equation, I guess."[2]

It is as if from time to time someone is destined to pop off, taking a shot, sometimes a cheap one, at Rodriguez, perhaps due to jealousy or because critics realize he tends to react rather passively, sometimes even agreeing with charges (e.g., he was playing poorly at a given time).

His former high school coach, Rich Hofman, elaborated on Rodriguez's deftness at avoiding controversy. "His public persona is different than his private; I think it hurts when people say those things to him. He also does take responsibility for his failures, and I think that's the first step towards becoming a great player and a great person; today kids are always making excuses and so are parents for the kids. One thing Alex didn't have was anybody to make excuses for him when he was young.

"He was always trying to do better; he was always thinking that he could do more, and I think that always served him well because a lot of kids today when they're told how great they are, that they're number one in the nation, they get careless, they start believing it and stop working. That [praise] just motivated him to do better."[3] In any case, early in spring training, Steinbrenner, still livid over Guillen's comments, vowed to take a more hands-on approach than he had in 2005. He boldly predicted, "We're going to win it [the World Series] this year. We're going after it." Aside from the probably unintended implication that they had not gone "after it" in previous years, the intent of his words was clear: He was reverting back to his attitude that failure would not be tolerated. Plus, in his mind the definition of failure was anything short of copping another gaudy World Series ring.[4]

Rodriguez was not on hand for some of the exhibition season as he, along with several other key Yankees, was competing in the WBC, which ran from March 3 to 20. He commented, "This may sound sentimental, but when I first reported and saw my uniform with 'Rodriguez 13' on the back and 'USA' on the front, I got the chills. It made me think of my brother, a 30-year veteran U.S. Air Force officer, and every other American I would be representing in this tournament."[5]

Going in, the United States was the event's favorite along with the Dominican Republic among the field of 16. Rodriguez seemed somewhat of a reluctant volunteer to play, in that he felt his preparation for the regular season was more important, and said he was "melancholy" about leaving the Yankees in the spring, "For me, spring training is such an integral part of what I do."[6]

In Round 1, A-Rod starred in the inaugural game, and then Team USA survived erratic play—including a shocking loss to Canada—to advance. After the March 12 Round 2 contest against Japan in Anaheim, Rodriguez commented, "It was the first opportunity of this sort I had, and that was definitely good. I definitely felt proud."[7] He was 7 for 14 at the time, including his two-out, seeing-eye single with the bases loaded in the ninth to scratch out a narrow 4–3 win, chasing home the winning run versus Japan.

Right around this time, one member of the media derisively called Rodriguez "Mister March," an obvious rap against him for hitting well early but not during postseason play.

Then Team USA bowed out when they could scratch out only one run, on a sacrifice fly, versus Team Mexico. Roger Clemens, a 341-game winner in the majors, absorbed the heartbreaking 2–1 loss, and Rodriguez coaxed a potentially key ninth-inning walk, only to be erased on a game-, and tournament-, ending double play. John Nadel observed of the team that went 3–3 on the tourney, "The outcome was a stunner considering Team USA fielded a line-up loaded with All-Stars."[8]

Shockingly, not only did the United States not advance to the finals, but the two teams that did so, Japan and Cuba, had a total of two players from major-league rosters on their squads: two for Japan, including Seattle's Ichiro Suzuki, and none for Cuba. Japan prevailed on March 20, 2006, with a 10–6 win over Cuba.

As camp broke, it was clear that, once more, Steinbrenner and General Manager Brian Cashman painstakingly had pieced together their own All-Star-caliber lineup. It was, in some respects, like the Frankenstein monster in that it was assembled from assorted "body parts" from other teams with a few homegrown products sprinkled in. It was an imposing figure that, outside of New York, was feared and loathed by many and possessed overwhelming power.

The Yankees were the Rodeo Drive of baseball. Tony Pena was on the coaching staff, having departed his job as the Kansas City Royals coach in 2005. The Royals payroll then stood at $30 million, not too much more cash than Rodriguez, at nearly $25.7 million, still the game's highest-paid player, would earn in 2006. In fact, the only starting player of the Yankees who would earn less than $10 million in 2006 was 23-year-old second baseman Robinson Cano. Since the Yanks had last won the World Series in 2000, Steinbrenner had spent $1 billion on his payroll. In a season in which the average player's salary was at nearly $2.9 million, Steinbrenner, with a $198.7 opening-day payroll—13 times more than the Florida Marlins payroll—was paying three Yankees more than $20 million a year, with Derek Jeter and Jason Giambi joining A-Rod in that group. Pitcher Mike Mussina's $19 million broke down to about $5,900 per pitch. The figures were staggering.

As a matter of fact, the 2006 crew's résumé was more lethal than the 1927 Yankees Murderer's Row band of sluggers that included Babe Ruth, Lou Gehrig, and two other future Hall of Famers.

Inked into the heart of the Yankees 2006 batting order, embedded in the cleanup slot, was Rodriguez. As the season opened, he was surrounded by talent such as the Yankees' new leadoff hitter Johnny Damon, wrenched from the roster of the Red Sox when he became a free agent, Jeter in the second spot, followed by hard-hitting Gary Sheffield, and protected by the number five hitter, Jason Giambi.

Toss out A-Rod's brief 1994 and 1995 seasons, and he had hit 424 big-league homers over 10 seasons. Thus, he entered the season virtually on the cusp of 500 round-trippers (with 429 total home runs). Reaching that strata would put him in the same exclusive circle of men as Hank Aaron, with his all-time high of 755 (being threatened by Barry Bonds), and Babe Ruth, who struck 714 shots. Certainly he was not about to swat 71 homers in 2006, but attaining the 500 plateau in 2007 was something to think about, and it helped put A-Rod's career in perspective.

Armed with two MVP trophies over the past three years and convinced that the 2005 season, a much better statistical season for him than 2004, established him as a bona fide Yankee, A-Rod felt very much at ease on the eve of the 2006 season.

After all, had he not become the first Yankees player to win the MVP award since Don Mattingly in 1985 and only the fourth player to win an MVP with two teams? That placed him among such all-time greats as Barry Bonds, who accomplished the feat with Pittsburgh and San Francisco, Jimmie Foxx of the Philadelphia Athletics and Red Sox, and Frank Robinson with Cincinnati and Baltimore.

Not only that, he had joined Hank Greenberg, Stan Musial, and Robin Yount as the fourth man to win the MVP while playing two different positions.

ANOTHER TURBULENT SEASON BEGINS

Heading into the new season, he clearly was pleased with, and bought into, the words of Torre: "He's getting more comfortable here in New York. Alex helped us win so many games, both offensively and defensively, and he continues to improve."[9]

Preseason publications touted Rodriguez's magnificence. Participants in fantasy leagues were advised, "He may be expensive, but you get what you pay for. No one puts up numbers like A-Rod at third base." He was the USA Today Sports Weekly pick as the best player in the game, still the king, commanding $44 in fantasy dollar value as compared to the $43 of Albert Pujols.[10]

As of opening day 2006, only four active players sported a career batting average of .300 or better with at least 400 homers to their credit. The elite group consisted of Barry Bonds at precisely .300 with 708 home runs,

Frank Thomas (.307, 448), Manny Ramirez (.314, 435), and Rodriguez (.307, 429).

If Rodriguez's performance in the April 3 opener was any indication, had A-Rod been any more "comfortable," he would have been comatose. He went three for five with five RBIs on a majestic grand slam and two singles in a 15–2 shellacking of Oakland.

On April 9, Rodriguez peppered a home run off Angels Bartolo Colon to open a five-run outburst in the second. The bazooka-like blow, his 431st, tied him with Cal Ripken Jr. for 37th place on the all-time home-run list. A week later, Rodriguez shot by Ripken, hitting number 432 in a 9–3 rout over the Twins.

On May 9, Rodriguez committed two costly errors, ones that led to five unearned runs for the Red Sox in their 14–3 rout. After the debacle, he was "singled out in quotes attributed to Steinbrenner," who stated, "I'm upset with a lot of them. The third baseman!" Typically, Rodriguez said he was unperturbed by the criticism and came back the next night with a homer off Boston's ace Curt Schilling.[11] Despite that blow, two nights later his home crowd booed him in his first two at bats. He responded with a homer his next trip to the plate and eventually went on to earn American League Player of the Month honors for May.

However, his May binge was followed by a June tailspin. By the middle of the month, Yankee hitting coach Don Mattingly mused that Rodriguez looked lost and was being booed in Yankee Stadium by fans, as relentless as they were unmerciful, "in almost every at bat," and harassed "because [of] a perceived failure in the clutch." After a loss on June 15, a seemingly unruffled A-Rod told reporters, "Rip away. Rip away. Rip away. If I was a writer, I'd probably be writing some nasty things. If I was a fan, I'd be booing me, too."[12] Matters were so bad that at one point Torre penciled A-Rod into the number five hole as Rodriguez's hitting woes lingered.

Eddie Rodriguez said Alex's attitude is, "You want to boo me, boo me. Sometimes people think that because they pay for a ticket [they can boo]. OK, you're allowed to boo, but I see kids five and six years old, 'Hey, you suck!' Five and six years old! And the father's standing next to him." A-Rod's former mentor feels one is certainly allowed to have an opinion, but buying a ticket does not entitle one to abuse a player.

Eddie feels the key to getting booed in New York is simple: "You've got the best baseball player in the world and you haven't won with him. I can understand people criticizing, but what I can't understand is people not appreciating a good baseball player." He said Alex's naysayers fail to credit him for his clutch play; for instance, in the 2004 American League Division Series "beating Minnesota by himself," allowing the Yankees to advance to play the Red Sox. Eddie feels critics "forget the first four games he played against Boston he was on fire." Then when he tapered off, he was singled out for his slump when, in reality, virtually the entire lineup tanked. "They didn't say anything about that. He just can do no right."[13]

Tom Grieve chipped in, "When you're a great player, especially now that [Alex] Rodriguez is on the Yankees and making that kind of money, I think the shock would be if he wasn't booed."[14]

On June 27 during a Yankees telecast, announcer David Justice, armed with stats, criticized Rodriguez's lack of clutch hitting. The next day, Rodriguez answered Justice with a game-winning, two-run homer. The very next game, in a you-just-cannot-win scenario, A-Rod popped up in his first at bat and Yankees fans again booed him.

On July 2, A-Rod, back in the cleanup spot, collected three hits, including two homers, good for seven RBIs in a lopsided 16–7 win over the Mets. Paul Lo Duca, the Mets catcher, miffed with A-Rod, feeling he had admired his grand slam a bit too much, yelled at Rodriguez, but nothing untoward transpired. Yankee fans disgustedly noted that 6 of his 19 homers were hit when the Yanks were ahead by or trailed by five or more runs.

That same day, Rodriguez was elected as the American League's starting third baseman for the midsummer classic, easily outpolling Boston's Mike Lowell by more than 1.1 million votes. "The whole world isn't in New York; there are some people out there who like me," Rodriguez said of the ninth time he was elected to start for the junior circuit, his 10th overall All-Star selection and his third start at third base. "I look forward to having fun representing the American League," said Rodriguez, a lifetime .316 hitter in All-Star play. "When so many fans vote for you, you have the responsibility to go out there and do your best."[15]

At the All-Star break, Rodriguez was hitting .282 with 65 RBIs and was hitting 24 points higher on the road than at Yankee Stadium.

In the game of July 17, Rodriguez committed three errors then shrugged off that single game nadir as a fluke. However, his 16 errors on the year represented the worst in the bigs for a third sacker, as was his .933 fielding percentage. In 2004 and 2005, he had combined for only 25 miscues.

Four days later, he became the youngest player to hit 450 home runs with the historic blast coming on his 2,000th hit. On the debit side, he was averaging one error per 5.1 games, an alarming rate, and on July 22 he whiffed four times as the Yanks designated hitter.

Around this time, Eddie Rodriguez pointed out that Alex was leading the league with RBIs that put his team ahead, but critics seem to ignore such assets. "I just can't wait until he wins a [World Series] ring. That's all that he's got on his mind. If he won a ring, he'd be unstoppable."[16]

By August 18, one negative facet of his game was glaring: His error total ballooned to 22, fourth worst in the majors, and the *Fox Sports Network Baseball Report* suggested he was "cracking under scrutiny," pointing to his poor glove work and his average, which was at its lowest since 1999. Commentator Ken Rosenthal said A-Rod should "stop worrying and let his talent flow" instead of issuing "public mea culpas." Rosenthal added that if Rodriguez could not quit fretting, the Yankee fans, predator-like, would sense his vulnerability and swoop down on him, exacerbating his problems.[17]

Tom Grieve analyzed Rodriguez's defensive play: "If you break down his tools, he's well above average in every facet of the game. If you go back forty or fifty years, shortstops were 5' 10" and 160 pounds, or they might have been like Mark Belanger, 6' 2" and 180 pounds [with] catlike quickness that you didn't see in players—and there weren't many players that were 6' 3" to begin with and 220 pounds like Alex. He's an incredible athlete. He has a well-above-average arm, he's an above-average runner, he has above-average hands at shortstop, above-average range to go to his right or left, and he makes the play coming in. There's only one defensive play that I wouldn't rate him above average, and that's going into the outfield after pop-ups. You have to look hard to come up with something he needs to really improve on. He never looked comfortable going back after a pop-up over his head. That is really nitpicking, but that's how good a player he is."

At third base, said Grieve in a March 2006 interview, Rodriguez has "all the same tools; he takes Gold Glove shortstop ability and just moves over to third base. He makes the play on the bunt, he makes fantastic diving plays in foul territory, and he's got a rocket of an arm to make off-balance throws. He's at the top of the list when you talk about defensive third basemen."[18]

Such praise made Rodriguez's poor glove work in 2006 even more astonishing, perhaps lending credence to the concept that his problems were more in his mind and mechanics, and it was, therefore, folly to believe his fielding skills had totally deteriorated.

The Yanks met Boston in Fenway for a five-game set from August 18 to 21 and swept them for a Boston Massacre Redux (recalling a similar sweep in 1978). It was just the second-ever five-game sweep by a first-place team over a club that began the series in second. Thus, the Yankees, who had been down by four games to Boston on Independence Day, took a six-and-a-half game lead and would never look back.

August found A-Rod in the batting doldrums, fanning 16 times over 28 at bats while stranding 19 runners. Then, mercifully, he snapped out of it. On August 31 and September 1, he was engulfed by the applause of capricious home fans demanding curtain calls.

So, in a season in which he found himself vilified, a season in which he led the league in errors and fanned 139 times, tying his career high, A-Rod still posted some big numbers, reaching 30 home runs, 100 runs, and 100 RBIs for the ninth straight year, tying the record shared by Jimmie Foxx and Lou Gehrig. He finished among the leaders in five major categories.

THE STING OF FAILURE

When the playoffs rolled around, however, none of that mattered. What did matter was the mighty Yankees, with All-Stars at *every* position, lost to Detroit in four and Rodriguez again failed in postseason play, hitting .071. Torre lost faith in him and dropped him to sixth, then *eighth* in the lineup, the lowest he had hit since May 7, 1996, when he was a 20-year-old.

Through 2006, Rodriguez had hit .098 with no RBI over his last 12 playoff games and was invisible with runners in scoring position. The querulous, fickle fans rained down boos on him, and the media called for him to waive his no-trade clause and to make like a villain in an old Western and get out of town by sunset. A-Rod said he refused to budge; he would prove his mettle in New York.

The media unabatedly called him a drama queen, a distraction, and self-obsessed. Yet, wrote Norman Chad, he remained "a drug-free, scandal-free superstar who doesn't embarrass himself. . . . He plays hard every day. And his reward for this? This year he's been booed at home . . . torched by the New York tabloids. . . . He is called E-Rod, K-Rod, and A-Fraud."[19]

After having spent almost $1 billion in salaries over the last six years, coming up empty once again was unpalatable to the Yankees, who fizzled, whimpered, and defied poet Dylan Thomas: They did go gentle into that good night.

NOTES

1. Mark Stewart, *Alex Rodriguez: Gunning for Greatness* (Brookfield, CT: Millbrook Press, 1999), 5.

2. Associated Press.

3. Author's interview with Rich Hofman, May 3, 2006.

4. *USA Today Sports Weekly*, March 1–7, 2006, 30.

5. Alex Rodriguez, "Arod's Journal," *AROD: The Official Site of Alex Rodriguez* (April 3, 2006), available at http://arod.mlb.com/players/rodriguez_alex/journal.jsp#april3.

6. *USA Today/Sports Weekly*, March 8–14, 2006, 22.

7. Associated Press.

8. Associated Press.

9. Associated Press.

10. *USA Today Sports Weekly Fantasy Guide '06*, Spring 2006, 14.

11. Associated Press.

12. Paul Hoynes, "MLB Insider," *The Plain Dealer*, June 18, 2006, C6.

13. Author's interview with Eddie Rodriguez, July 6, 2006.

14. Author's interview with Tom Grieve, March 8, 2006.

15. Mark Feinsand, "Four Yankees Score All-Star Selection: A-Rod, Jeter elected by fans; Cano, Rivera picked by players," *The Official Site of the New York Yankees* (July 2, 2006), available at http://newyork.yankees.mlb.com/news/article.jsp?ymd=20060702&content_id=1534866&vkey=news_nyy&fext=.jsp&c_id=nyy.

16. Author's interview with Eddie Rodriguez, July 6, 2006.

17. *FSN Baseball Report*, August 18, 2006.

18. Author's interview with Tom Grieve, March 8, 2006.

19. Norman Chad, "Too Many Worms in the Big Apple," *The Plain Dealer*, October 3, 2006, D2.

Chapter 10

RODRIGUEZ'S FEATS, KUDOS, AND HIS LEGACY

Texas third base coach Steve Smith recalled managing Rodriguez in the minors where he quickly spotted what would become obvious to all. "You knew with the talent that he had that it was going to be a matter of time with him getting up [to the majors] and doing it. So then he went right up [from Smith's Triple-A Calgary club], and the rest is history."[1]

As early as July 1997, with fewer than 300 games under his belt, Rodriguez had so impressed George Will, he wrote, "The Yankees' brilliant twenty-three-year-old Derek Jeter may never be the American League's best shortstop, so gifted is the Mariners' twenty-year-old Alex Rodriguez."[2]

During the latter half of the 1999 baseball season, Major League Baseball conducted fan voting to select the All-Century Team. Although no Latino player made the cut, writer Tim Wendel sought out experts in order to select an informal Latino All-Century squad. He approached Omar Minaya, the first Latino general manager of a big-league team. Minaya commented, "You have to start with Alex Rodriguez . . . or Vladimir Guerrero." Aside from the outfield position, there were more great Latin shortstops selected, six, than any other position.[3]

In 2004, all-time great Rickey Henderson said he was so taken with Alex Rodriguez that, although he had great respect for Barry Bonds, the one matchup of active players that he liked to watch the most was A-Rod versus Pedro Martinez—a battle of the bests. Two years earlier, Texas manager Jerry Narron concisely summed up what Henderson felt, calling A-Rod "the best player in the game."[4]

Once, Rangers teammate Michael Young spoke of his awe for A-Rod, then coming off a torrid streak in which he had amassed eight hits over his last nine at bats. Young compared the ease with which Rodriguez hits to the seemingly routine skill of a young, master videophile. "We're playing baseball and he's playing video games, up there pushing buttons and doing whatever he wants."[5]

Outfielder Brad Wilkerson, sounding much like a pitcher, said the best way to defend Rodriguez is to "keep the guys off base in front of him—not giving him the opportunity to come up with that big, three or four RBI hit, because you give up a solo home run, you still have a chance to win a game. Any dangerous hitter is hard to contain, they're going to get their hits eventually. They're going to have ups and downs like anybody, but their downs are a little bit less than the others."[6]

When a pitcher has to face Rodriguez, his feelings, according to Texas righty Kevin Millwood, border on trepidation. "He's just an intimidating guy at the plate; he can do so many things—he can hit the ball out of any place of the park, he makes contact, he's tough to deal with every time he comes to the plate." Although A-Rod is not exactly huge, Millwood says that "in a lot of ways he is a big, burly slugger. He can do so many other things to beat you, so keeping him off the bases is a big deal."

Further, although Rodriguez no longer steals 30 bases or so, Millwood said, "You always have to be conscious of him; you can't just leave him alone over there. It's just another way he can wreak havoc while you're on the mound."[7]

In 2006, Cleveland manager Eric Wedge said the one word that best sums up A-Rod is "consistent. He plays everyday, going to put up a good at bat every time he goes up there, and he's somebody you have to respect from day to day as a player." He liked his consistency "with his routine and with his approach to the game. From year to year, series to series, he's the same guy in terms of what we see on the diamond. Obviously he has as much ability as anybody in the game." Wedge added that with the talent A-Rod has surrounding him, "it's tough to pitch around the guy, but you ultimately know that if you make a mistake, he's going to hurt you."[8]

Catcher Rod Barajas added, "With a guy like that, you just got to hope he's not on a hot streak because when he's on a hot streak, there's nothing you can really do to get him out. You have to go on the scouting reports, you have to look at his swing—see what kind of swing he takes."[9]

Rodriguez also has the all-important but rare ability to hit well with two strikes. In 2004, then all-time saves leader Lee Smith rattled off the active players he believes are the best in this realm, listing Barry Bonds.

Although he also mentioned Manny Ramirez and Gary Sheffield, the name he came up with immediately after Bonds was A-Rod.[10]

A-ROD'S SWING AND ITS RESULTS

Obviously, much of Rodriguez's success begins with his cut, a swing somewhat reminiscent of Brady Anderson's, with A-Rod's right hand coming off the bat as he completes his swing, with the left hand remaining to hoist the bat high after his long, arching cut. "A lot of guys [have that type of swing] nowadays," observed Michael Young. "It just seems like it's in vogue now for guys to hit that way, but whatever way guys feel they're getting the best extension, getting to the ball the best, that's the way they're going to hit." That extension leads to numerous home runs; the swing comes straight out of the Charlie Lau theory of hitting.[11]

When asked what type swing A-Rod has, Barajas quipped, "Deadly. That's all I see. It's powerful; he's got just as much power as anybody in this game. I don't think there's anybody that might have more power than him. He's strong enough where even if he doesn't hit the ball on the sweet spot, he's able to hit it out of the park. He's definitely got a little swoop in there, and that's why he hits all those home runs—he likes getting that ball in the air."[12]

Although uppercuts and big swings often result in strikeouts, both Barajas and Rodriguez's high school coach, Rich Hofman, say they certainly can be justified. Hofman noted that the strikeouts are part of the package that comes with power hitters but conceded, "I guess if there's one thing that always bothers me is the strikeouts—I don't think he likes [them] either. Everything else about his game is great. If one day you're going to be the best home run hitter of all time, I guess you're going to have to go for the big swing almost every time. I understand what the deal is—I mean, the strikeouts equals home runs, and batting average equals lack of strikeouts.

"I really feel like if he concentrated on just making contact and hitting to all fields like he did when he was 18 years old and he won the batting title, I think he could hit .400. So it's a conscious decision that you have to make in order to determine what you're getting paid to do. I'm sure he feels like he's being paid to hit home runs and drive in runs, and the sacrifice is sometimes not cutting down on your swing a little bit with two strikes."[13]

Barajas added, "If you want those rewards, you're going to have to go through that. Usually most of your power hitters are striking out close to the 100 mark; it's just part of the game. You want somebody to strike out less than 30, 40 times, you're going to get a contact hitter. With those great players, you definitely overlook the strikeouts just so you can get the rewards from all the home runs."

Rodriguez, said Barajas, thrives by hitting "mistakes. That's basically the key to hitting, being able to take advantage of the mistake that a pitcher makes. If he leaves a fastball over the plate, it doesn't matter if it's 87 or 96 [miles per hour], if you're ready for a fastball and he leaves it where it's definitely hittable, he can do some damage with it. Hanging slider? Same thing.

"There are times when whoever is hitting behind him, if they're not swinging the bat as hot as he is, you'd definitely rather face the guy behind him so you're gong to pitch him a little more carefully."[14]

Texas pitcher Kevin Millwood further analyzed, "Right now he seems to me he's got his own kind of swing, and it's a swing that works really well for him." Although he considers the cut to be rather big and looping, "It's definitely not slow." Rather, his light saber of a bat, slashing through the strike zone, is sleight-of-hand quick.[15]

Hofman said of A-Rod's so-called long swing, "I don't think it was that way in high school. I think he developed the Charlie Lau philosophy at first. Now it's probably a combination of whatever he's decided and how he feels comfortable."[16]

Millwood added that all players "go through streaks where they can't hit a certain pitch, but what makes him so good is he's able to adjust to that quicker than most people." Thus, in a game in which adjustments are critical, A-Rod stands out.[17]

THE A-ROD LEGACY

The legacy of Alex Rodriguez will be evaluated in many ways: his talent and his ranking in the annals of baseball and the true measure of a man, his character and what he leaves behind, including both literal and figurative gifts he bestowed upon others.

When it comes to judging Rodriguez the player, praise flows plentifully. When Rodriguez was 24 years of age, Texas Rangers scout Rudy Terrasas commented that he was one of those rare players who can "beat you in all facets of the game," be it his running, his glove work, or his power.[18] As big-league hitting instructor Jeff Manto said of another talented player, such sluggers have "the power to shrink any ballpark."[19] Plus, Terrasas was impressed that Rodriguez still had a "tremendous upside." Most baseball players who had accomplished what A-Rod had already achieved were typically pushing the 30-year-old level. He concluded with an understatement, observing that if he were building a team and was in need of a shortstop, Rodriguez was that man.[20]

In 1998, former outfielder Dave Henderson, who went on to become a broadcaster with the Mariners, lauded Rodriguez, too. He contended that A-Rod had somehow gone *beyond* being a five-tool player. He was impressed with how, after pitchers made their adjustments to him, Rodriguez came right back, adjusted to them, and continued to amaze everyone. "That signifies greatness," said Henderson. "There's no fluke in this man's game." Another former teammate, Rich Amaral, also admired Rodriguez's marvelous instincts, which particularly help when running the bases.[21]

As far back as 1996, Cal Ripken Jr. recognized how great Rodriguez would become. He gushed to *The Sporting News* that probably all Alex would need was "experience to become the shortstop everyone else will be watching in our league." He added that "the future belongs to Alex Rodriguez."[22]

Six years after Ripken made his glowing comments, none other than Hall of Fame shortstop turned first baseman Ernie Banks upped the ante. He not only called Rodriguez the best shortstop of them all, but he also elaborated, "To see this young man play that position with his power and his defensive ability, it's really, really exceptional." He gave the nod to Rodriguez over himself due to A-Rod's strength and over Ripken Jr. because of his superior power numbers.[23]

Like Banks, Rodriguez's achievements were so deserving of kudos, he even won an MVP trophy while playing for a loser. A-Rod's 2003 sensational season earned him the baseball equivalent of a papal imprimatur: He won the MVP with the last-place Rangers.

Continuing comparisons with Ripken Jr., beginning relatively early in Rodriguez's career, had been as inevitable as they were highly flattering. Again, from as long ago as 1996, Cleveland General Manager John Hart commented in a *Sports Illustrated* piece that both men were large shortstops and very physical. Hart even went so far as to state that Rodriguez might be "a better athlete."[24]

Larry Bowa, an All-Star and Gold Glove Award recipient who went on to manage in the majors, said that Rodriguez continued to get stronger yet already had outstanding power. He said he could not fathom what Rodriguez would eventually wind up achieving.[25] By 2005, Rod Carew commented that he felt A-Rod was the game's best hitter, and Paul Molitor said that when discussing the elite, "You look for guys that have that combination of power and average and are still able to do situational things."[26]

Incredibly, in December 2003, when there were rumblings that Boston's acquisition of Rodriguez was imminent, Red Sox Kevin Millar was asked if it were up to him, would he select current teammate Nomar Garciaparra or A-Rod to best help out the team, he publicly stated his pick was Rodriguez. Although he tipped his cap to Garciaparra as a two-time batting champ, he added, "When you're looking at an all-around great player who can hit fifty home runs, drive in 140, and possibly, obviously, win a batting title . . . [w]ith his defense, A-Rod is the best in the game."[27]

"[Mark] Belanger was the Gold Glove shortstop in the American League when I was playing," commented Tom Grieve. Alex Rodriguez is as good as Belanger was defensively and he's going to have offensive numbers that are second to none when he retires. It's like taking the best power hitter in the lineup and the best shortstop defensively 30–40 years ago and putting them together in the same player, and you've got Alex Rodriguez."[28]

WHAT THE FUTURE MAY HOLD

Although accurately projecting a player's current statistics into the future at any stage of his career is a nearly impossible task, it is, nevertheless, an entertaining process. Rodriguez refuses to get caught up in such prognostications, saying, "The most important thing is now. Looking ahead is contrary to what I'm about."[29]

Still, based on his stats through 2006 and factoring in the concept that ballplayers' stats wane in their latter stages, here are some educated guesses as to where Rodriguez might finish his career, assuming he does not hang up his cleats until he reaches the age of 40, five seasons after his current contract expires after the 2010 season. The 3,000-hit strata should be reached with ease, and he may even attain about 3,500 to 3,600 hits to crack the top five of all time. Two thousand RBIs is a realistic goal, with Hank Aaron's record of 2,297 feasible if A-Rod can average approximately 106 RBIs over the next nine seasons. It should be noted as a yardstick that through 2006 Rodriguez, a lifetime .305 hitter, had averaged 43 homers and 125 RBIs per 162 games played.

Author Elliott Kalb believes Rodriguez could finish with as many as 800 lifetime homers, usurping the records of Babe Ruth, Bonds, and even Aaron, and has a "great chance" to reach 700, shattering through that barrier the way Chuck Yeager broke the sound barrier: with a resounding boom.[30] Based solely on mathematics, when Rodriguez was still 30 years of age, with a home run total nearing 450, it was projected that he would eclipse Aaron's 755 homers in 2014 at the age of 39.

Practically speaking, though, is it feasible? Tom Grieve thinks so. "Yep. Here's why. I think he can hit 40 home runs every single year well into his 30s. He started out when he was so young and he keeps himself in impeccable condition and he's never been hurt. If other players can play into their late thirties and early forties, I can't imagine he won't be one of them." Barring injuries, Grieve said, "I see that drive, kind of like Nolan Ryan who pitched into his forties probably because of personal goals and the love of the competition. Alex is the same way."[31]

As Cleveland manager Eric Wedge put it in 2006, "With the pace that he's on right now, when he's all said and done, it could be pretty special stuff."[32]

Michael Young concurs that a healthy Rodriguez should put up lifetime numbers to rival the Aarons of the game. Young's capsule comments of Rodriguez were: "Just a great all-around player. Does it all. Does it on the field and plays to win."[33]

All-Star catcher Ivan Rodriguez agrees, calling for A-Rod to become the all-time home run king if he remains healthy. "His swing is always there, he's always driving the ball." Furthermore, Detroit's Brandon Inge cited A-Rod's uncanny ability "to read pitches better than anybody. . . . He anticipates so well, he figures out patterns."[34]

In an April 2006 interview, Brad Wilkerson said, "What he's brought to the game, he's kind of lurking in the shadows under Barry Bonds and all the talk about Bonds right now, but [Rodriguez] is close to 500 home runs already and he's only 32 [he was actually only 30 at the time of the interview]—he's got a lot of years left. He's a guy that can really do some damage to the home run race. He's just an all-around great athlete; it's amazing how many home runs he's hit, and guys these days are keeping themselves in such great shape, he's strong, he's still running very well. It's going to give him longevity and the opportunity to break a lot of records."[35]

His success should be no shock because he had already ranked as the top home run hitter of all time by 27, 28, 29, 30, and 31 years old.

Most experts' projections for A-Rod's final stats rank him with men such as Lou Gehrig, Ted Williams, Babe Ruth, and Hank Aaron. The humble Rodriguez always had stated that he found it an honor to be considered in the same realm as baseball's all-time greats. "Most of the names," he confessed, "ring a bell. . . . I'm only human, so I'm tickled to be mentioned with them, compared with them."[36]

Asked to play word association, Rich Hofman's response to "Alex Rodriguez" was, "The greatest."[37] Tom Grieve summed it up: "A uniquely talented ballplayer who is perfectly prepared physically and mentally to always be at the top of his game."[38] Bill Henderson's reply was, "focused, and to expound upon that, I think his talent got him to the big leagues, but to be the superstar and future legend that I think he'll be, he has a work ethic and desire to be the best that I've never experienced with any guys I knew or played with. That's saying a lot about a person when there's a lot of guaranteed money coming your way. He's also a real inquisitive guy. To this day, to a lesser degree, he's always asking questions."[39]

Eddie Rodriguez said Alex is a person with strong morals, constantly giving, and that his on-the-field destiny is just as impressive, saying he is on his way to become "the greatest to put a uniform on."[40]

THE INTANGIBLES

It would be easy, perhaps even tempting, for some players who have achieved as much as Rodriguez has to become complacent, to bask in his glory. That is simply not his style.

Exactly how he will be viewed after he retires depends upon which facet one explores. It is obvious how others think of Alex Rodriguez the hitter and shortstop. As for being a team leader, some say he has come up a bit short in that respect. He has insisted that he is the type of relatively quiet player, such as a Hank Aaron, who leads by example, relying upon his performance and work ethic to speak for him and to help motivate teammates to stronger performances. He once stated that the role of a leader is one a player has to earn and that, for example, with the Mariners, he had earned a leadership mantle with his productivity and attitude. In short, he stated, "When it's all over and done, I want to go down being remembered as a winner."[41]

In Texas, Rafael Palmeiro unequivocally said Rodriguez was the leader. "He's the man here. We rise and fall with him. . . . He's proving to be a great leader, too." Rodriguez concurred, saying he felt the responsibility to "turn around this team" was palpable.[42]

Tom Grieve concluded, "When he was with the Rangers, he was a leader in every way: on the field with the way he played the game, and he was a vocal leader in the clubhouse, a take-charge kind of guy all the way.

"I think it will probably take him a while to assume that role with the Yankees because he's got so much respect for the game and the other players and he knows that he can't just go into the Yankee clubhouse where Bernie Williams, [Derek] Jeter, [Jorge] Posada, and all those guys who have been there for a long time and won championships and be the guy that takes over and is a vocal leader. He's the kind of guy who knows how to act in every situation. He's never going to be embarrassed. How he's perceived is very important to him."[43]

A final way to gauge the man has nothing to do with sports. "Forget about baseball," said former Seattle teammate Stan Javier. "If my son was that old [all grown up], Alex is how I'd want him to be. . . . He's a good man."[44]

Another former teammate, outfielder Ricky Ledee, who was with Rodriguez in Texas, called Rodriguez, "the best teammate I've ever had."[45]

Dr. Claudia Springer, who taught Alex in high school, said, "I have students ask frequently about what kind of a student Alex was, but they are looking for spectacular stories. The truth is that he was diligent, polite, and thorough. Not too exciting for 17-year-olds who are looking for some foreshadowing of greatness! I just wish more of them understood how much diligence, good manners, and hard work goes into being a great athlete."[46]

"Whoever would've told you that Alex Rodriguez would be this great— he's lying," mused Eddie Rodriguez. "Everybody knew he'd be a good major leaguer—good, but not this great. I'll tell you this: When he gets a uniform on, he's special. He tries to be the best; he doesn't want to be second to none. It kills him when he leaves a man on base, it kills him he hasn't won a ring, and it killed him the first time they robbed the MVP from him."[47]

Linda Warner commented that she and her husband, Paul, teachers at Westminster Christian, have nothing but "good things to say because we both loved him and enjoyed him as one of our all-time favorite kids," and added that he was "a delight as a student."[48]

In *Heart of a Champion,* a chapter dealing with the quality of excellence featured Rodriguez. Clark Kellogg, former NBA player and current television analyst, was quoted as saying that people should "not settle for 'good' versus 'best.'" He added that, at times, there is a tendency to convince ourselves that we have indeed done the best job possible, but, in truth, we had been content merely to have done rather well. As Kellogg pointed out, however, Rodriguez possesses all the traits that a person in his situation should have, such as his great work ethic, his humility, his faith, his munificence, and his refusal to forget his roots.

"He has millions of dollars in the bank, millions of fans in the stands, and millions of admirers who would like to be him.

"He is baseball's answer to Tiger Woods, Kobe Bryant, and Jeff Gordon.

"He is young, handsome, articulate."[49]

As author Glen Macnow put it in 2002, "He is a star for the next generation—tall, graceful, good-looking, and well spoken." He cited a *Newsweek* article that rued the recent retirements of superstars such as Michael Jordan and Wayne Gretzky and pondered who could replace such luminaries. *Newsweek* mentioned three candidates: Tim Duncan, Tiger Woods, and Rodriguez.[50]

Rodriguez's said that if such a comparison also came with the same type of success Jordan had, that was fine with him. Quite revealingly, however, he added that he did not crave glamour.[51]

It is noteworthy that throughout all the hype and amid all the kudos, Rodriguez has remained levelheaded. Take, for example, the fact that despite his diligence and performance, Rodriguez refuses to take credit for his superlative prowess, telling *The Sporting News*, "I really feel like I've been given this gift, that I've been blessed."[52]

Additionally, throughout all the lavish compliments he has received, he realizes that there have been some offsetting criticisms, albeit mostly picayune ones. Therefore, he continues to downplay both the praise and the rancor.[53] His refusal to get caught up in the hype stems from his mother, who told him "not to brag about his baseball talents" at an early age.[54]Though far from finished with his career, Rodriguez has had to face some scathing charges that he has yet to win the World Series. In fact, after Boston won the 2004 series, Curt Schilling went a step beyond that. "If we get A-Rod [before the 2004 season], we don't get [to the World Series], I don't question that for a second."[55]

Tom Grieve bristles at the contention that Rodriguez is not a true winner because he owns no World Series rings. "Those kinds of arguments hold no value, and they're almost ludicrous. You hear them say, 'He's never won a Super Bowl.' Well, does that mean that Dan Marino is not as good a quarterback as [Brad Johnson] was with Tampa Bay when they won it? There have been a lot of mediocre players on World Series teams, and to say that Ernie Banks wasn't as good a player because he didn't play in a World Series—I don't buy that argument. The best sport to make that argument would be basketball because one player can impact a team more.

"The one sport where it's the most ludicrous argument is baseball because look at the three years that Alex had in Texas and we ended up in last place every year. He couldn't even impact our team to get us out of last place. One player *can't* do that. An All-Star lineup can't win with bad pitching. So the argument that he is less of a player because he's never played in and won a World Series makes absolutely no sense."[56]

When Gary Sheffield learned that his Yankees had signed Rodriguez, he blurted, "It's over. It's over. There's nobody in the game that can beat us now."[57] He was, of course, soon proved to be wrong. In short, there are no guarantees in baseball.

After all, other greats—21 Hall of Famers, ranging from George Sisler and Nap Lajoie to Rod Carew—never played in a World Series. As a matter of fact, back in 1997 when Rodriguez first felt the anguish of losing in the playoffs, he muttered, "Hopefully I'll be on the other side celebrating some time in my career."[58] Through 2006, his lamentations continued.

SUMMING UP THE LEGACY

In another realm, A-Rod's legacy as a man, and a philanthropist at that, lives on in many places. At Westminster Christian High School he is a saint, having established a scholarship fund there. He was, quite naturally, named to the school's baseball Hall of Fame.[59] He unfailingly continued his work as a national spokesperson for his beloved Boys and Girls Clubs of America, donating generously, $500,000, to the club he had attended in Miami.

Further, he often visits schools where he, with preacherlike intensity and sincerity, lectures on the harms of smoking, using drugs, and drinking alcohol. In 1996, he originated a program he dubbed Grand Slam for Kids. The program was designed to encourage children to focus on schoolwork, to become good citizens, and to pay heed to their physical fitness.[60]

Then, in 1998, he set up the Alex Rodriguez Foundation, with numerous clubs established to "teach children to care for their community as well as themselves." His foundation also donated a chunk of money to victims of Hurricane George, which had battered the Dominican Republic. His largest display of largesse came six years later when he bestowed close to $4 million to the University of Miami to rebuild their baseball facility, which now is fittingly named Alex Rodriguez Park.[61] As a kid, Rodriguez had, on occasion, sneaked into the university's baseball stadium.[62]

As an avid reader (often voraciously consuming motivational books by writers ranging from basketball's Pat Riley to Anthony Robbins),[63] Rodriguez stressed that he not only realizes the importance of learning, but he also passes on that insight to youngsters.

If the measurement of money is tossed into the equation, although certainly Rodriguez himself would rather be judged by different criteria, he stands tall. According to a baseball Web site, through 2006 he had earned, solely through his baseball salaries, a mind-boggling $147,707,727 over his career.[64] Contrast that to, say, the amount earned by Babe Ruth during a different era, and the gap is staggering. Roger Kahn wrote that Ruth's lifetime baseball income was $1,076,474, with an additional $1 million or so in auxiliary earnings.[65]

Those in Rodriguez's camp are convinced that had he not made the switch from shortstop to third base, he would have ended his career considered to be the greatest shortstop in the annals of the game. Perhaps that does not bother Rodriguez himself in that his goal is to emerge as the greatest player ever, regardless of position played.

Before their marriage, Cynthia Scurtis tried to sum up just who Alex Rodriguez is. "People fall in love with his image. . . . They love the idea of Alex. They love his smile." She knew he was a heartthrob but said she trusted him unquestioningly, "[A]ll you have to do [to trust him] is know him."[66]

Buck Showalter contends that due to all of Rodriguez's good deeds, he truly deserves a squeaky-clean image, "But we all try to shoot at things like that. I don't know what it says about our society, but it's the sports world we live in today and, unfortunately, all phases [of life], because there is such a networking of information and there aren't that many people willing to think for themselves and go, 'OK, hold on a second, what do I know about this guy and what do they know?' When I get new players, I tell people, 'Listen, let me make up my own mind.' There aren't that many people willing to do that, they all want to network. It's so easy to go along with public perception. I mean, Alex, I always marvel that all the hoopla and the pressure on him and how he continues to perform at a very high level. The games are always a haven to those types of talented people."[67]

In 2005, *The Sporting News* put out a book listing their top 100 players of all time. A-Rod was their 70th selection but was rising with a bullet. They called him "a new-generation, five-tool prototype who has been choreographed for success." They also singled him out for "his near-perfect mechanics, durability, instincts and career numbers. . . . [H]e's the 6–3 slugger with the DiMaggio stride and blazing bat speed who drives pitches to all fields."[68]

Mark Teixeira, who played in the same infield with A-Rod for one season, called Rodriguez "probably the most talented players in the game. Physically, one of the most impressive players I've ever seen." He then, perhaps better than anyone, captured the essence of A-Rod, "He's one of those guys born to play baseball."[69]

Author Tim Wendel said that "a grinning Rodriguez is another example of the ballplayers who have become the new face of baseball."[70]

It seems clear that Rodriguez's face may not always be a smiling one, especially in light of recent tribulations, but it is equally clear that his generosity is unquestioned. Also, he already has put up numbers that shine as brightly as klieg lights at a Hollywood premier. Therefore, he is considered by many to be the heir apparent to the throne; he may very well end his career as the greatest baseball player ever.

NOTES

1. Author's interview with Steve Smith, April 2003.

2. George F. Will, *Bunts: Curt Flood, Camden Yards, Pete Rose and Other Reflections on Baseball* (New York: Scribner, 1998), 288.

3. Tim Wendel, *The New Face of Baseball: The 100-Year Rise and Triumph of Latinos in America's Favorite Sport* (New York: HarperCollins, 2003), 205.

4. Associated Press.

5. Associated Press.

6. Author's interview with Brad Wilkerson, April 28, 2006.

7. Author's interview with Kevin Millwood, April 28, 2006.

8. Author's interview with Eric Wedge, April 28, 2006.

9. Author's interview with Rod Barajas, April 28, 2006.

10. Author's interview with Lee Smith, April 2005.

11. Author's interview with Michael Young, April 28, 2006.

12. Author's interview with Rod Barajas, April 28, 2006.

13. Author's interview with Rich Hofman, May 3, 2006.

14. Author's interview with Rod Barajas, April 28, 2006.

15. Author's interview with Kevin Millwood, April 28, 2006.

16. Author's interview with Rich Hofman, May 3, 2006.

17. Author's interview with Kevin Millwood, April 28, 2006.

18. Michael Bradley, *Alex Rodriguez* (Tarrytown, NY: Benchmark Books, 2005), 32.

19. Paul Meyer, "For Pirates Power Prospect, It's All about Contact," *Pittsburgh Post-Gazette,* March 18, 2006, D3.

20. Bradley, *Alex Rodriguez,* 32.

21. Mike Shalin, *Alex Rodriguez: A+ Shortstop* (Champaign, IL: Sports Publishing, 1999), 69, 70.

22. Michael A. Pare, *Sports Stars, Series 3* (Detroit: UXL, 1997), 246.

23. Bradley, *Alex Rodriguez,* 7.

24. Pare, *Sports Stars,* 246.

25. Bradley, *Alex Rodriguez,* 8.

26. Gordon Wittenmyer, "The Art of Hitting," *Baseball Digest,* July 2006, 42.

27. Mike Vaccaro, *Emperors and Idiots: The Hundred-Year Rivalry between the Yankees and Red Sox—From the Very Beginning to the End of the Curse* (New York: Doubleday, 2005), 187.

28. Author's interview with Tom Grieve, March 8, 2006.

29. *USA Today Sports Weekly,* May 12–18, 2004, 14.

30. Elliott Kalb, *Who's Better, Who's Best in Baseball?* (New York: McGraw-Hill, 2005), 71.

31. Author's interview with Tom Grieve, March 8, 2006.

32. Author's interview with Eric Wedge, April 28, 2006.

33. Author's interview with Michael Young, April 28, 2006.

34. Tom Gage, "A-Rod Does it Better," *Baseball Digest,* October 2005, 24.

35. Author's interview with Brad Wilkerson, April 28, 2006.

36. Steve Riach, *Heart of a Champion: Profiles in Character,* with John Humphrey (Nashville, TN: Broadman and Holman, 2001), 14.

37. Author's interview with Rich Hofman, May 3, 2006.

38. Author's interview with Tom Grieve, March 8, 2006.

39. Author's interview with Bill Henderson, July 2006.

40. Author's interview with Eddie Rodriguez, July 6, 2006.

41. Jeffrey Zuehlke, *Alex Rodriguez* (Minneapolis, MN: Lerner, 2005), 28.

42. Wendel, *The New Face of Baseball,* 202.

43. Author's interview with Tom Grieve, March 8, 2006.

44. John Hickey, "Alex Rodriguez Not a Typical Superstar," *Baseball Digest,* July 2000, 40.

45. Joe Christensen, *Alex Rodriguez* (Edina, MN: ABDO, 2004), 5.

46. E-mail correspondences with Dr. Claudia Springer, May 2006.

47. Author's interview with Eddie Rodriguez, July 6, 2006.

48. E-mail correspondences with Linda Warner, May 2006.

49. Riach, *Heart of a Champion*, 1, 12.

50. Glen Macnow, *Sports Great, Alex Rodriguez* (Berkeley Heights, NJ: Enslow, 2002), 8.

51. Ibid., 10.

52. Pare, *Sports Stars*, 247.

53. Bradley, *Alex Rodriguez*, 38.

54. Zuehlke, *Alex Rodriguez*, 12.

55. Devin Clancy, "When We Last Left These Two Rivals," *USA Today Sports Weekly*, April 6–12, 2005, 4.

56. Author's interview with Tom Grieve, March 8, 2006.

57. John Kuenster, "A-Rod and Jeter May Become Best Duo Ever on Left Side of Infield," *Baseball Digest*, June 2004, 21.

58. Bill Koenig, "Early Exit Leaves Mariners with Sour Taste," *USA Today Baseball Weekly*, October 8–14, 1997, 40.

59. Zuehlke, *Alex Rodriguez*, 13.

60. Marylou Morano Kjelle, *Alex Rodriguez: Professional Baseball Player* (Hockessin, DE: Mitchell Lane, 2006), 25–26.

61. Ibid., 26.

62. Wendel, *The New Face of Baseball*, 202.

63. David Nemec and Saul Wisnia, *100 Years of Baseball* (Lincolnwood, IL: Publications International, 2002), 493.

64. Sports Reference, Inc. "Alex Rodriguez," *Baseball Reference* (2007), available at http://www.baseball-reference.com/r/rodrial01.shtml.

65. Roger Kahn, *Beyond the Boys of Summer* (New York: McGraw-Hill, 2005), 70. Please note that *The Sporting News*, August 25, 1948, stated Ruth's total baseball salaries were $925,900. To give some comparison, in 1918 the most expensive ticket for the World Series cost $3.30; in 2006 the *cheapest* ticket ran $90 and box seats were $250. Ruth lived in an era when a yearly salary of about $4,000 was sufficient for a person to live in a big house, have a car, and comfortably raise a family.

66. Jim Gallagher, *Alex Rodriguez: Latinos in Baseball* (Childs, MD: Mitchell Lane, 2000), 60.

67. Author's interview with Buck Showalter, April 28, 2006.

68. Ron Smith, *Baseball's 100 Greatest Players*, 2nd ed. (St. Louis: The Sporting News, 2005), 152.

69. Author's interview with Mark Teixeira, April 28, 2006.

70. Wendel, *The New Face of Baseball*, 203.

BIBLIOGRAPHY

BIOGRAPHIES AND AUTOBIOGRAPHIES OF ALEX RODRIGUEZ

Bradley, Michael. *Alex Rodriguez*. Tarrytown, NY: Benchmark Books, 2005.

Christensen, Joe. *Alex Rodriguez*. Edina, MN: ABDO, 2004.

Covert, Kim. *Alex Rodriguez*. Mankato, MN: Capstone Press, 2002.

Gallagher, Jim. *Alex Rodriguez: Latinos in Baseball*. Childs, MD: Mitchell Lane, 2000.

Kjelle, Marylou Morano. *Alex Rodriguez: Professional Baseball Player*. Hockessin, DE: Mitchell Lane, 2006.

Macnow, Glen. *Sports Great, Alex Rodriguez*. Berkeley Heights, NJ: Enslow, 2002.

Pare, Michael A. *Sports Stars, Series 3*. Detroit: UXL, 1997.

Rappoport, Ken. *Super Sports Star Alex Rodriguez*. Berkeley Heights, NJ: Enslow, 2004.

Rodriguez, Alex, and Greg Brown. *Hit a Grand Slam*. Dallas: Taylor, 1998.

Shalin, Mike. *Alex Rodriguez: A+ Shortstop*. Champaign, IL: Sports Publishing, 1999.

Stewart, Mark. *Alex Rodriguez: Gunning for Greatness*. Brookfield, CT: Millbrook Press, 1999.

Stout, Glenn. *On the Field With . . . Alex Rodriguez*. New York: Little, Brown, 2002.

Thornley, Stew. *Alex Rodriguez: Slugging Shortstop*. Minneapolis, MN: Lerner, 1998.

Zuehlke, Jeffrey. *Alex Rodriguez*. Minneapolis, MN: Lerner, 2005.

BOOKS ON BASEBALL HISTORY

Goldman, Steven, ed. *Mind Game: How the Boston Red Sox Got Smart, Won a World Series, and Created a New Blueprint for Winning*. New York: Workman, 2005.

Harris, Cecil. *Call the Yankees My Daddy*. Guilford, CT: Lyons Press, 2006.

Jensen, Don. *The Timeline History of Baseball*. New York: Palgrave Macmillan, 2005.

Kahn, Roger. *Beyond the Boys of Summer*. New York: McGraw-Hill, 2005.

Nemec, David, and Saul Wisnia. *100 Years of Baseball*. Lincolnwood, IL: Publications International, 2002.

Olney, Buster. *The Last Night of the Yankee Dynasty*. New York: HarperCollins, 2004.

Ribowsky, Mark. *The Complete History of the Home Run*. New York: Kensington, 2003.

Schlossberg, Dan. *The Baseball Almanac*. Chicago: Triumph Books, 2002.

Shaughnessy, Dan. *Reversing the Curse: Inside the 2004 Boston Red Sox*. New York: Houghton Mifflin, 2005.

Stewart, Wayne. *Fathers, Sons, and Baseball: Our National Pastime and the Ties that Bond*. Guilford, CT: Lyons Press, 2002.

———. *Hitting Secrets of the Pros: Big-League Sluggers Reveal the Tricks of Their Trade*. New York: McGraw-Hill, 2004.

Stout, Glenn. *Yankees Century: One Hundred Years of New York Yankees Baseball*. New York: Houghton Mifflin, 2002.

Suárez-Orozco, Marcelo M., and Mariela M. Páez, eds. *Latinos Remaking America*. Berkeley and Los Angeles: University of California Press, 2002.

Vaccaro, Mike. *Emperors and Idiots: The Hundred-Year Rivalry between the Yankees and Red Sox—From the Very Beginning to the End of the Curse*. New York: Doubleday, 2005.

Wendel, Tim. *The New Face of Baseball: The 100-Year Rise and Triumph of Latinos in America's Favorite Sport*. New York: HarperCollins, 2003.

Will, George F. *Bunts: Curt Flood, Camden Yards, Pete Rose and Other Reflections on Baseball*. New York: Scribner, 1998.

BOOKS ON SPORTS FIGURES

Kalb, Elliott. *Who's Better, Who's Best in Baseball?* New York: McGraw-Hill, 2005.

Riach, Steve. *Heart of a Champion: Profiles in Character*. With John Humphrey. Nashville, TN: Broadman and Holman, 2001.

Smith, Ron. *Baseball's 100 Greatest Players*. 2nd ed. St. Louis: The Sporting News, 2005.

STATISTICAL REFERENCES

Aust, Dave, Pete Vanderwarker, Tim Hevly, and Bob Wickwire, eds. *1994 Seattle Mariners Information Guide*. Seattle, WA: Mariners Baseball Club, 1994.

Bower, Jeff, Clay Davenport, Jeff Hildebrand, Gary Huckabay, Rany Jazayerli, Chris Kahrl, Keith Law, et al. *Baseball Prospectus: 2001*. Dulles, VA: Brassey's, 2001.

Neft, David S., Richard M. Cohen, and Michael L. Neft. *The Sports Encyclopedia: Baseball*. 23rd ed. New York: St. Martin's Griffin, 2003.

———. *The Sports Encyclopedia: Baseball*. 25th ed. New York: St. Martin's Griffin, 2005.

The Sporting News. *The 1995 American League Red Book*. New York: The Sporting News, 1995.

DOCUMENTARY FILMS

Major League Baseball Superstars Show You Their Game. Produced by Major League Baseball Productions, 2005.

MAGAZINE ARTICLES

Clancy, Devin. "When We Last Left These Two Rivals." *USA Today Sports Weekly*, April 6–12, 2005, p. 4.

Gage, Tom. "A-Rod Does It Better." *Baseball Digest*, October 2005, p. 22.

Hickey, John. "Alex Rodriguez Not a Typical Superstar." *Baseball Digest*, July 2000, p. 41.

Kepner, Tyler. "Alex Rodriguez's Talent Has No Boundaries." *Baseball Digest*, May 1999, pp. 34–35.

Koenig, Bill. "Early Exit Leaves Mariners with Sour Taste." *USA Today Baseball Weekly*, October 8–14, 1997, p. 40.

Kuenster, John. "A-Rod and Jeter May Become Best Duo Ever on Left Side of Infield." *Baseball Digest*, June 2004, pp. 17, 20.

Livingstone, Seth. "Questions Surround AL East Powers." *USA Today Sports Weekly*, October 12–18, 2005, p. 46.

———. "Yankees Getting Cranky, Creaky." *USA Today Sports Weekly*, 20–26 April 2005, p. 29.

Lockwood, Wayne. "Mariners' Alex Rodriguez: Standing Tall at Short." *Baseball Digest*, July 1997, p. 40.

Lowe, John. "Aiming to be the Best." *Baseball Digest*, October 1999, p. 47.

Nightengale, Bob. "House of Ruth Shaken to Foundation." *USA Today Sports Weekly*, October 27–November 2, 2004, pp. 11–12.

———. "New Look, Same Personality." *USA Today Sports Weekly*, April 26–May 2, 2006, p. 11.

———. "Yankees Dynasty Hanging by a Thread." *USA Today Sports Weekly*, June 15–21, 2005, p. 6.

"Players with the Best Skills." *Baseball Digest*, August 1998, p. 50.

Post, Paul. "Ozzie Smith Rates Alex Rodriguez Best All-Around Player in Majors." *Baseball Digest*, May 2001, p. 37.

Stone, Larry. "Shortstop Star Power." *Baseball Digest*, May 2001, p. 35.

USA Today Sports Weekly, May 12–18, 2004, p. 14.

USA Today Sports Weekly, June 1–7, 2005, p. 15.

USA Today Sports Weekly, June 8–14, 2005, p. 14.

USA Today Sports Weekly, March 8–14, 2006, p. 22.

USA Today Sports Weekly Fantasy Guide '06, March 1–7, 2006, p. 14.

Verducci, Tom. "A-Rod Agonistes." *Sports Illustrated*, September 25, 2006, pp. 37–44.

Wittenmyer, Gordon. "The Art of Hitting." *Baseball Digest*, July 2006, p. 42.

ONLINE ARTICLES

Associated Press. "Players In Majors Born Outside U.S. Jumps." *Puerto Rico Herald*, April 7, 2005. Available at http://www.puertorico-herald.org/issues2/2005/vol09n14/Media1-en.html.

"A-Rod's new deal: No more clubs." *ESPN.com*, November 14, 2005. Sidebar. Available at http://sports.espn.go.com/mlb/news/story?id=2223736.

"Brien Taylor." *Wikipedia: The Free Encyclopedia*, February 2007. Available at http://en.wikipedia.org/wiki/Brien_Taylor.

Feinsand, Mark. "Four Yankees Score All-Star Selection: A-Rod, Jeter elected by fans; Cano, Rivera picked by players." *The Official Site of the New York Yankees*, July 2, 2006. Available at http://newyork.yankees.mlb.com/news/article.jsp?ymd=20060702&content_id=1534866&vkey=news_nyy&fext=.jsp&c_id=nyy.

"Major League Baseball and Chevrolet Unveil Program Celebrating the Greatest Latino Players in the History of the Game." *General Motors Corporate Website*, August 23, 2005. Available at http://www.gm.com/company/gmability/community/news/chevy_mlb_082305.html.

Martone, Art. "A-Rod: Friendship with Jeter has 'cooled'." *Providence Journal: Projo Sports Blog*, February 19, 2007. Available at http://www.beloblog.com/ProJo_Blogs/sportsblog/2007/02/arod_friendship_with_jeter_has.html.

"Report: A-Rod warned about playing poker." *NBCSports.com*, November 2, 2005. Available at http://www.msnbc.msn.com/id/9896335/.

Rodriguez, Alex. "Arod's Journal." *AROD: The Official Site of Alex Rodriguez*, April 3, 2006. Available at http://arod.mlb.com/players/rodriguez_alex/journal.jsp#april3.

————. "Arod's Journal." *AROD: The Official Site of Alex Rodriguez*, April 3, 2006. Available at http://arod.mlb.com/players/rodriguez_alex/journal.jsp#april3.

Snow, Chris. "Award lands in A-Rod's glove." *Boston Globe*, November 15, 2005. Available at http://www.boston.com/sports/baseball/redsox/articles/2005/11/15/award_lands_in_a_rods_glove/.

Sports Reference, Inc. "Alex Rodriguez." *Baseball Reference*, 2007. Available at http://www.baseball-reference.com/r/rodrial01.shtml.

NEWSPAPER SOURCES

Associated Press

Chad, Norman. "Too Many Worms in the Big Apple," *The Plain Dealer*, October 3, 2006, D2.

Hoynes, Paul. "MLB Insider." *The Plain Dealer*, June 18, 2006, C6.

Meyer, Paul. "For Pirates Power Prospect, It's All about Contact." *Pittsburgh Post-Gazette*, March 18, 2006, D3.

TELEVISION SHOWS

FSN Baseball Report, August 18, 2006.

INDEX

About the Author

WAYNE STEWART has now written more than twenty books and countless magazine articles. He was born and raised in Donora, Pennsylvania, a town that has produced big-league baseball players, including Stan Musial and the father-son Griffeys. Mr. Stewart has covered the baseball world since 1978 and has interviewed and profiled many Hall of Famers, including Nolan Ryan, Bob Gibson, and Warren Spahn. He has appeared, as a baseball expert, on Cleveland's Fox 8 and ESPN Classic.